SEND THIS MESSAGE TO MY CHURCH:

Christ's Words to the Seven Churches
of Revelation

BY

Terence Kelshaw

THOMAS NELSON PUBLISHERS
Nashville • Camden • New York

Copyright © 1984 by Terence Kelshaw

All rights reserved. Written permission must be secured from the publisher to use or reproduce any part of this book, except for brief quotations in critical reviews or articles.

Published in Nashville, Tennessee, by Thomas Nelson, Inc. and distributed in Canada by Lawson Falle, Ltd., Cambridge, Ontario.

Printed in the United States of America.

Unless otherwise noted, Scripture quotations are from the NEW KING JAMES VERSION. Copyright © 1979, 1980, 1982, Thomas Nelson, Inc., Publishers.

Scripture quotations marked RSV are from the Revised Standard Version of the Bible, copyrighted 1946, 1952, © 1971, 1973.

Library of Congress Cataloging in Publication Data

Kelshaw, Terence.
  Send this message to my church.

  1. Seven churches.   2. Bible. N.T. Revelation II-III—
Criticism, interpretation, etc.   3. Christianity—20th
century.   I. Title.
BS2825.2.K45   1984   228'.06   84-3484
ISBN 0-8407-5897-9

FOR MY MOTHER
who taught me to be a Christian

CONTENTS

SEND
THIS MESSAGE
TO MY CHURCH

INTRODUCTION

For years I have struggled with the state of the church. Modern Christians often see it as optional; clergy despair over its lack of vitality and what can be done to correct it.

The various churches described in the New Testament appear, for the most part, to be a mixture of healthiness and apathy all at once. Although things are rarely perfect in the church, the gates of hell do not prevail against her either. So we need to have abundant faith, and yet maintain realistic expectations.

The seven churches in the book of Revelation have always intrigued me in this regard. "I would give anything to visit them, see the locale of those churches, and try to learn better what the church has been and what she can be again," I would muse to myself.

One night, at about 11:30 P.M., I answered the telephone to hear a friend ask if I would like to visit Turkey.

I revealed my ignorance by asking why a group of Christians would want to visit Turkey, attempting to stifle my excitement behind a placid voice.

My clergyman friend whistled through his teeth in undisguised disgust. "That's where the sites of the seven churches of Revelation happen to be," he answered. "Come as guest speaker. Eighteen months should give you plenty of time to prepare."

My inquisitive mind, questing nature, and the nagging

fear that I might "miss something" all began to function at once. It was something I simply had to do!

We traveled from my then home in Bristol, England, through France, Germany, Austria, Yugoslavia, Greece, across the Bosphorus into the world of the East, to Turkey, and then back again via Bulgaria—upwards of seven thousand miles—and shared wonderful experiences. Our visit to each of the seven sites of the churches in Revelation 2 and 3, with open Bible in hand, began to teach me life-changing lessons about renewal for the church.

My thanks are expressed to Mrs. Grace Cowlin who typed the original material for the tour, to Kathleen Blight who performed a mammoth task of translating it into material for publication, and to Mrs. Edith Kleisley, Mrs. Ruth Crick, Mrs. Diann Peck, and Mrs. Dorothea Wessner who shared in the typing for final presentation to publishers. Without the help and encouragement of Mr. Peter Gillquist, senior editor for the publishers, and the constant encouragement of my wife, Hazel, from the original right through to final manuscript, and the patience of my four children, Julian, Joanne, Rachel, and Michael, who allowed me to take time from a special family holiday in Florida to do some writing, this book would still be in the stage of sermon notes. Finally, I would like to acknowledge the man on the other end of the telephone, the Reverend John Walden, who planned this journey in extraordinary detail, with not one mistake or timing hazard, as light relief from his main occupation as a parish minister.

My prayer is that in reading this book one might thrill to the possibilities open to that believer who submits to the sovereign lordship of Jesus Christ in His church.

Ambridge, PA
Winter, 1983

Chapter 1

THE STATE
OF TODAY'S CHRISTIANITY:
Being Honest with Ourselves

Write the things which you have seen, and the things which are, and the things which will take place after this (Rev. 1:19).

The Orient Express steams into the main station at Istanbul after its long journey from Paris, its opulent china and magnificent silver now carefully stowed away. Its passengers, each with a special story to tell, gather their goods, call a porter, and set off to their hotels. Tonight they will gingerly wander about the city—by the waterfront where fishermen still cook fresh fish in the sterns of their boats, through the small crooked back streets of the town, and around that magical, dazzling, bustling bazaar—if it is still open. This place has a warmth and fragrance all its own.

Certainly tomorrow they will go in search of the mystery, the grandeur, the excitement of a city made famous, attractive, and even compelling in Agatha Christie's famous novel. The visitors may find no such similar excitement and mystery; but they most certainly will find cultural enchantment, ancient history, and a myriad of taxis!

A boat ride on the Bosphorus is the best way to view the skyline at Istanbul. The ancient domes and minarets stand rather majestically among the twentieth-century buildings. It is their mystery and age that captivate and lure the visitor into the city. A significant part of that skyline is a particularly large dome, still unequaled in its claim to be among the largest unsupported structures in the world. Here is the church of Holy Wisdom, called simply Saint Sophia.

LIGHT IN DARKNESS

Until the third century a pagan temple stood on this site, but when Christianity was established as the official religion of the Eastern Empire in A.D. 314, the emperor Constantine erected a magnificent basilica, its enormous unsupported dome a wonder in the world. Istanbul at that time was called Constantinople; and Saint Sophia, the first official church building, stood as a permanent reminder of the struggle that had accompanied the church into birth. It was a church that had been established by the blood of the martyrs.

Life was still far from easy for Christians, and the emperor Constantine issued many orders and entered into much correspondence in their defense. When reporting his meeting with Emperor Licinius in what is now known as the Edict of Milan, he wrote,

> . . . we decided that of the things that are of profit to all mankind, the worship of God ought rightly to be our first and chiefest concern.[1]

Establishing a day of worship in another edict in A.D. 321, he wrote,

> All judges, city people and craftsmen shall rest on the day of the Sun . . . so that the opportunity afforded by the divine

[1] H. Bettenson, *Documents of the Christian Church* (London: Oxford University, 1963) p. 16.

providence may not be lost, for the right season is of short duration.[2]

The church began to grow stronger. To be sure, it was accompanied by much debate and not a little amount of heresy; but it withstood them and matured in the battles of its own conflicts, marching ever onward in the faith of Christ crucified. It had, as the reformers were to say in a later age, "a goodly heritage." That heritage was the apostolic faith rooted in the centrality of the Incarnation: the birth, life, death, and resurrection of Jesus Christ. It was a preached faith, which transformed a continent, an empire, and eventually the whole world as it left its mark on peoples and society.

The Christian is mindful of the tragic events created by the church in every generation when, having forgotten its apostolic call to preach the gospel of peace and salvation, it has marched to battle for a lesser cause or political issue. The world, for its part, must also be mindful of the great humanitarian work of the church in every society through the ages. Its clergy and people have sacrificed and labored to bring healing, education, civilization, and even political and economic growth to this planet. Through the twists and turns of an often tortured and lost world, the gospel of peace and reconciliation has won through to bring healing and security to nation and individual.

So it is today.

One only has to see the poor Christians in Uganda, whose poverty itself is a present reminder that the Christian church aligns itself with the deposed and the undertrod, to recognize that God's people derive from their spiritual Source that strength which gives to others purpose

2Ibid., p. 18.

and courage. In the Western world, one need only take a glimpse at the Christian relief organizations, the missionary support systems in less fortunate areas of the world, and the sacrificial giving and service of Christians everywhere who come to the aid of an often battered and bruised world community, to recognize that the church seeks constantly to be in the forefront of international care and support, bringing with it the good news of God's saving grace.

The gospel of peace and reconciliation is based in the knowledge that Jesus Christ is moving among the churches to speak His word and encourage His church to be honest with itself. Often we are not honest. Often our faith becomes fixed in something other than union with our Lord Jesus Christ. Often we substitute faith in God with religious practice and doubtful affiliations. And when we do, we are challenging that truth in which Saint Paul was so firmly established when he claimed that God's grace was sufficient for all things.

The church through the ages has often fallen into the trap of believing it could help God's work of reconciliation along by reinterpreting it for its own generation. When it does that, it demonstrates its own weakness and futility and suggests that God's grace is not sufficient for all things.

FOOD FOR THE FED-UP

You may well ask, "What has all this to do with the contents of two chapters of perhaps the strangest and least understood of all the books of the Bible?" And, in fact, why focus attention on seven little-known cities of the ancient world of which only one, Ephesus, is mentioned significantly anywhere else in the New Testament? What can they possibly have to do with keeping the twentieth-century

16

church honest in its proclamation of a gospel of peace and reconciliation?

We could also ask, are those seven churches mentioned in Revelation 2 and 3 sufficiently important to warrant our special attention anyway? Can we really accept a view that would tell us that in the latter half of the twentieth century there is something significant we sophisticated moderns may learn from our first-century Christian predecessors?

You know, of course, that my answer will be a resounding yes. The German theologian Dietrich Bonhoeffer once described the church as "a redeemed piece of the world," and I respond to that idea vibrantly. Because the church is such, it must be committed to examining itself in the light of Scripture and of its being called to be honest with itself. It is in that sense of honesty that Jurgen Moltmann in his book *The Church in the Power of the Spirit* affirms,

> The church's first word is not "church" but Christ. The church's final word is not "church" but the glory of the Father and the Son in the Spirit of Liberty.[3]

What he is saying is this: we do not exist for ourselves; neither does the church for itself. While it is true that we always live in that tension of individual faith on the one hand and the community of believers on the other, we are called to follow Christ and glorify the Father, Son, and Holy Spirit in whatever practical actions of faith and service the church finds before it. There is no privatization in Christianity. All Christians are in the church and part of it. We find ourselves asking, "Then what is the function and ultimate justification of the church?" Karl Barth would answer,

[3]Jurgen Moltmann, *The Church in the Power of the Spirit* (New York: Harper & Row, 1977) p. 9.

"The church *is* mission," which itself sounds fine and is certainly quite true; but the people of God gathered together for mission must first of all learn from God and be equipped in the power of the Spirit to proclaim the gospel.

Learning from God and being equipped in the power of the Spirit to proclaim the gospel entails equally as much dealing with the challenges that came to our Christian predecessors as it does rejoicing in their victories. For that reason, I sense there is much more in the messages to the seven churches than even we who value the Holy Scriptures often recognize. In an age that tends to think that today's Christians have more spiritual light than those early followers of Christ, there are important challenges here to the whole Christian community.

If Bonhoeffer was correct in describing the church as "God's redeemed piece of the world," looking at ourselves with honesty becomes important. Sometimes that is only possible by looking at ourselves reflected in others.

Let the churches of Revelation, then, be our mirror. And again, let us dare to believe that there are important challenges in these chapters not only to the whole Christian community of our time, but also to the nature of our existence as a church and our operation of ministry. Questions like "Why are we here?" "What are we doing?" "Where is our foundation?" "What are we communicating to the unbelieving world?" "What is the church's value and purpose?" find substantial answers in what Jesus Christ had to say to the church of the first century.

It is my intention to examine in each of the letters a brief history and background of the city. Then, using the geographical and historical data as a backdrop to discover—rather like a detective putting clues together to form a full picture—something of what was taking place in the churches and of why Jesus Christ spoke the messages He did. Finally I wish to apply His message to our own situation.

THREE OBSERVATIONS

First I want to make three general observations about Christian experience, which were as common in church life in the first century as they are in our time.

As I worked with the biblical material, and often as I spent time at one or another of the sites, a recurring question nagged at my mind. How could it be, with all the great apostolic oversight those early Christians received from such giants of the faith, that they should be in need of such a terrifying divine visitation? How is it possible that any of those churches could become as deceptively weak in faith and ministry as five of the seven appear to have been? What was happening to them? Worst of all, could it *really* happen to us? Those questions will be the focus for my observations.

1. Earthly Christianity Is a Constant Temptation

It is to Martin Luther we owe the phrase "Peace if possible, but truth at any rate." I wonder what were John's reactions to the command, "Write the things which you have seen, and the things which are, and the things which will take place after this" (Rev. 1:19), because such a command posed for him some ethical questions. You see, the churches in the area thought of themselves as being fairly much at peace, but the truth was that the "things which are" left much to be desired; and honesty in the situation would most certainly create problems for the people in those congregations. At best John would be described as negative and at worst fraudulent in his claims to the visions.

Speaking to oneself, being honest with oneself, means

19

dealing with the tendency to denial, like the cancer patient who says when death is imminent, "I don't want to know what I have." If we don't know, perhaps it won't happen; and we can pretend for a little longer. When I must deny about myself, then I can deny about my neighbor as well, and I don't need to know what my neighbor has or does not have. I can imagine my neighbor and myself out of historical existence and into a "forever family," in which "forever" becomes not an affirmation but a denial. And I suspect that as John wrote, he was addressing that kind of denial.

What he saw could not have filled the heart of that pastor of the flock with great joy; yet it was exactly what he saw that led him to go on to write the encouragements he did. What he saw cannot be limited to the church in his own age, for it has surfaced in every generation; and the church must keep speaking to itself in order to avoid the pitfalls. He was dealing with that which is also painfully evident in our own day.

There is a brand of manmade theology that has made a fine art the practice of accommodating the gospel to fit the age in which it finds itself, in much the same way as did John's church. It is a theology that challenges God with an attitude of "How far can I go from the center of the faith and still call it Christian?" I call this "earthly Christianity." It is a Christian faith that appeals to God but is made in the image of man. That is to say, humankind is seen as the very center of God's concerns and activity, so He is required to react to human will and demands. God on the end of a string, you might say.

Although such Christianity claims divine source, it operates almost totally at the level of human need and response, seeing God as the ever working, ever patient manager of a cosmic supermarket. We are the consumers. Entry into the cosmic supermarket is a coupon called prayer. The goods in the supermarket are all free and are intended to keep the shopper happy by supplying continuously every want.

I am being, perhaps, a little severe. Dietrich Bonhoeffer said it much better:

> The essence of grace, we suppose, is that the account has been paid in advance and, because it has been paid, everything can be had for nothing. Since the cost was infinite the possibilities of spending it are infinite. What would grace be if it were not cheap? Cheap grace means forgiveness of sins proclaimed as a general truth; the love of God taught as a Christian "conception" of God. An intellectual assent to that idea is held to be of itself sufficient to secure remission of sins. [4]

Saint John was facing directly the issue of manmade theology. Bonhoeffer faced it for a world racked with the hate and agony of war, challenging the church against creating a gospel without a cross or a Christianity that was made more in the image of man than the image of God. My first observation is that in the church we also are going through a replay of the situations faced from John's day through to the present. Being honest with it could be painful.

The tragedy is this: When one talks in terms of earthly Christianity, most of us immediately relegate that to what has become known as religious humanism. But the truth is, my dear brothers and sisters in Christ, that God is *still* issuing in these letters a warning against such apostasy beamed at what we would call today "Bible-believing, born-again Christianity." This biblical mail is also addressed to *us*.

2. An Experiential, Contentless Gospel

The age in which Saint John lived was an age of survival for most people and particularly so for Christians. We, too,

---

[4]Dietrich Bonhoeffer, *The Cost of Discipleship* (New York: Macmillan, 1963) p. 45.

live in an age of survival, much of it created by greed and inhumanity, some by political subterfuge. For many, Christianity becomes a way of escape through the preaching of a man-centered Christianity, which of itself lays the false foundation for the cosmic supermarket Christianity with which we have been dealing.

It is the Christianity of a contentless gospel that forms my second observation about the church. The contentless gospel is high on experience and, like all manmade theology, tends to perceive God on a string, ready and able to do all that is required, but at human direction. In a sad way the contentless gospel has become good news for an age of survival, because it allows the individual to be the sole controller of life and destiny.

The preachers of this gospel, many of them totally dependent on their own charisma and organizational ability, promise that there is a simple answer to the needs and hurts experienced in life, implying that God is primarily concerned with the areas of hurts and needs, real or imagined. The formula is simple. Simply repeat a set of words, get involved in a church, and learn the language. Repeat that language continually, especially in the hearing of others who have followed this formula, and here is the answer to the pressures of life and the hurts that destroy.

Some Christians call this legal fiction. Dietrich Bonhoeffer called it cheap grace:

> Cheap grace is the grace we bestow upon ourselves. . . . it is the preaching of forgiveness without requiring repentance, baptism without church discipline, communion without confession. Cheap grace is grace without discipleship.[5]

[5]Ibid., p. 45.

22

"Formula Christianity," with its contentless gospel, is dependent on new experiences to keep faith alive. It is a gospel without a cross (though the cross might be a central "selling point") and tends to lead to activism as a way of convincing oneself, or to experiential faith as a way of "topping up" the decision made. It is a verbal Christianity dependent upon key phrases or repetition of preachers' sayings.

Instead of being an answer to the hurts and pains of life, such Christianity becomes an anesthetic, and one of two things appears to take place. The anesthesia wears off, and the new Christian falls away from what he thinks to be the gospel and tries to cope with "hurts" in other ways. Or the language of earthly Christianity is adopted, and some measure of activism keeps the formula alive. When one arrives at a level where it appears to be working, one has unwittingly bought into deception.

I have found something interesting about this kind of Christianity. It exists totally for the recipient. This faith resides in the brain, depends on a preacher's activating impulses, and will always talk spiritualities provided one is never expected to translate that into action—except action that is easy to manage and will in the long term (or better still the short term) benefit the church image and membership.

C. H. Spurgeon, himself a great communicator and very popular preacher, was well aware of the danger and often warned his seminary students against becoming so popular that they be forced to preach a popular gospel also. For a popular gospel is death.

The contentless gospel overemphasizes one aspect of the gospel. It seems, for example, to be obsessed by eternity, but regularly disdains orthodox doctrine, careful scriptural exposition, and recognition of God the Holy Spirit at work in any way other than a given formula.

It may seem strange that such verbal Christianity, being cerebral, should so disdain doctrinal orthodoxy or scriptural accuracy. But by verbal Christianity we do not mean the intellectual pursuit of faith that might lead to growth. The contentless gospel is cerebral in that it is a mental assent to a set of words that, through constant repetition, assures the speaker of Christian faith. On the principle that if you say a thing often enough you may come to believe it, religious rhetoric (relating how God, by fulfilling felt needs, is thereby meeting the faith of the speaker) becomes a necessary "arm of the flesh."

The root of the trouble is something we might call "decision Christianity." The recipient, having made a decision in accord with the formula presented to him, is assured of having received freely a new life—a way of escape from the old and membership in a new family, a forever family, whose sole purpose is eventually to rejoice together in heaven. But presently it denies reality.

This is not new to our age. It is a man-centered theology that was also found in some of Saint John's churches. Among some of the more "exciting" elements, such theology produced complacency and compromise. It produced the "cheap grace" gospel, about which the theologian-martyr Bonhoeffer found himself writing in his generation. And there is a great deal of it in the church today, which is why the letters of Revelation are still important to us.

3. The Enemy Often Looks Good

Another way of escape in an age of survival, and this forms my third observation, is to take on some identification with the predator.

I once had an interesting encounter with a chameleon. It

was perched on the rusty colored branch of a tree. I had been sitting for some time on a grassy bank nearby before I noticed the chameleon; but now I spotted it through its movement, hunting for flies. In the meantime, another animal settled on the branch; and what happened to the chameleon was interesting. To this point it had not changed its color totally, for there had been no particular threat. But once the danger appeared, the chameleon took on total likeness to the rusty-brown branch until it was indistinguishable from it. It froze there until the danger was past.

Some people in John's churches were doing just that. Partly as a survival technique, individuals and even whole congregations began to rest on the branch of paganism, so to speak; and when the predator of Roman provincial power came along, or punitive threats for being Christian were handed out, the chameleons were about to change color so that they were no longer identifiable. Such chameleonlike behavior in a largely pagan population meant making faith and worship, creed and practice, words and action so acceptable to themselves and "outsiders" that no one could possibly be offended. It was a case of "the end justifies the means," and the Christians so involved would think Luther out of his mind with his "Peace if possible, but truth at any rate."

You see, it was important in those days of survival to discover a road of acceptability; and since the easiest option was to take on some identification with the enemy, that justified the kind of actions and strange belief systems that were being propounded in the name of Christ and His church. That kind of nominal Christianity, which is always searching for acceptability—that "middle road"—in fact, weakens Christian faith. "Chameleon" Christianity tends to be concerned that experiences, especially in any communal exercise like worship, should be at least as good as any comparable exercise in the world of unbelievers. In this experience, how the worshiper *feels* is of the greatest importance. Here is a theology that begins with human need, pride, self-esteem, and emotional appetite. God's word can wait! Such experience-centered faith is not at all concerned with orthodox belief and worship, but with "how I feel"; and thus it tends to judge personal daily relationships with God at this level. Dangerously so!

THE SUBTLETY OF DEATH

Strangely enough, many churches do not realize that they are taking on identification with the predator. This is why such behavior is called deception. To illustrate, let me tell you a true story. I once visited a worship service that began in a traditional manner but soon gathered momentum in an atmosphere of excitement. Make no mistake, I prefer my worship out of the oven rather than the refrigerator and this service had all the promise of lively worship. It was a church to which most members came from many miles away, happily ignoring any idea of being "salt of the earth" in their own neighborhoods, in exchange for the "exceptional worship experience."

Their expectations were certainly rewarded, as I discovered. The leader of the worship service moved his congregation from song, to chorus, to song with clapping, to chorus with hand and body action. Hands raised heavenward, people in the congregation prayed. Someone read a parable as a dance group moved into action in a vivid and beautiful visual portrayal. There was much talk of community, belonging together, Christian peace, and leading the world to Christ. We were told to say hello to each other,

26

but I was a visitor and did not belong to one of the many groups there. I stood self-pityingly alone.

The singing accompanied the preacher into the pulpit; and I prepared for some strong expositional direction for life—perhaps some words of challenge or just some thought for comfort. What we got was a "nationwide" sermon, which drove an uncharted course through the Bible, visiting as many lightly connected texts as possible. The sermon was liberally spiced with personal achievements and unconnected funny tales—more a performance than a preaching. It was a set of Christian thoughts held together by random stories. But it seemed not to matter, since the content was of less importance than the "party experience," and it was now warm and glowing with great atmosphere. Divine revelation mattered little in the wake of the dynamic feeling both service and preacher now evoked.

The purpose of the service was to make the *experience* so great that the worshiper would bring others, probably from a "less lively" church, to help the congregation "grow." Like the teen-agers' rock concerts, the experience counted more than content. It certainly was warm and exciting in that church, but as I left and stepped into the frosty night, the sharp cold wind seemed to cut through me, and I was alone.

Another example of how "experiential faith" takes on identification with the enemy is much more insidious.

Tom and Joan were ordinary, believing folk. Joan's husband, Ed, was not a Christian, and their relationship, though good, had been often strained because of Joan's Christianity. Tom was a man in mid-forties who had come to faith in Christ directly as a result of the death of his wife. Tom and Joan got to know each other and formed an adulterous relationship. Eventually they visited a minister.

The purpose was to ask whether it was right to pray for Ed to desert Joan so that she and Tom could marry! No, there was nothing wrong with Joan and Tom's relationship, and the adultery could be overlooked, they said, because (a) they had met as a result of their Christian faith, (b) Tom understood Joan better than Ed did, (c) surely the gospel is about love and they did love each other in a way they had never loved before, and (d) since life was very happy for them both, this was a fulfillment of what God wanted for people. He wants us to be happy and contented, doesn't He? Whatever the means, these stories suggest, God wants us to be happy in the end.

Such experiences and justifications were exactly what John found himself writing about in his correspondence with the churches of which he was the minister. The three observations I made concerning the church at the end of the twentieth century were to be observed also in the church at the end of the first century: manmade theology, a gospel without content, and a religion dependent on experiences. The manmade theology supposes God to be at the end of a string and in the service of humankind; the gospel without content is satisfied with a formula for faith; the "experience-centered" faith is so dependent on feelings that Christianity becomes an excitement drug, keeping one going from week to week or crisis to crisis.

IS FEELING BETTER WORSE?

What's so wrong with being lively, anyway? What can be so bad about the kind of worship service just described?

Its weakness lies in the dangerous assumption that if we can make Christian experiences better than those outside the church, we can show that God really is concerned primarily for human happiness. It doesn't take seriously the truth that all experience is momentary. Neither does it deal with the objective truths about God in relation to His people.

Let me tell you the rest of the first story, because it leads to where so many other similar experiences in the church lead. A group in the church became very dissatisfied, largely because they had traveled the gamut of experiences the fellowship had to offer and were now ready for "the deeper things of God." They were not unlike Thyatira, really, with a strong and self-reliant leader. They formed their own study group, an innocent enough procedure, but after a while they severed from the church to do their own thing, a not-so-innocent procedure.

One morning we were about to leave for vacation when a knock on the door sent a groan through the household. Standing at the door was a student friend who looked as if he had seen a ghost. In a way I suppose he had.

The previous night he had met with this dissident group of believers, whom he knew, and had accepted an invitation to join them in a great experience of faith as they searched for the deep things of God. It turned out to be a full-blown occult worship based on the understanding that if some "truth" made them feel good it must be from God. Their reliance on experience had led them far astray of a scripturally-based gospel.

It was much the same in the churches of the Revelation. There were some who never capitulated to compromise or followed the latest religious fashions. Some struggled against mockery from fellow believers and suffered at the hand of unbelievers but would not accommodate the gospel to the sway of the situation. Jesus was always finding those who had kept His name, and to all but two of the churches He opens His letter with commendation and affirmation. Even where He does have hard things to say it is always in the context of repentance and a promise of victory and fulfillment.

You see, much Christianity can so easily be little better than Christian humanism, a theology made by man and designed for nothing better than to heal life's hurts and make life better. God intends *so* much more for us.

Here were people in the heat of fire. They were under incredible daily pressure where words, experiences, or an idea about God would not greatly help. Many took the easy way of escapism, accommodating the gospel with such pagan practices as might save their necks. Much, though not all, of what is in Revelation 2 and 3 speaks to that. But much is couched in terms of victory and encouragement to those whose sole confidence was in Jesus Christ. Though it was difficult to see that in what was happening, God intended their good, they held on to the truth that "My grace is sufficient for you" (2 Cor. 12:9). Battered and torn in the fray, they found comfort in the remembrance of Jesus' words, "Come to Me, all you who labor and are heavy laden, and I will give you rest" (Matt. 11:28).

THE WORD WE LOVE TO HATE

Over and over again in the messages to these seven churches comes the call, *Repent*. Let go of all the trappings of your self-centered life and submit to the lordship of Jesus Christ. The call of Christ is not to a better existence but to a different existence, not to decision about Him but submission to Him. The gospel does not bring us to a head knowledge but to a heart faith. It brings us to a God who is in control, who is never taken by surprise and whose grace is sufficient in the darkest days.

And because there is no shortcut to Christian discipleship and holiness of life, it is a call that cannot circumvent the church. It is a call Christ presents to His church for a costly and sacrificial discipleship of mind, will, and possessions.

The churches under the oversight of Saint John were warned against adopting a culturally conditioned gospel, a gospel that made no challenge to the culture, a gospel centered almost totally upon answering human problems and hurts. They were challenged instead by a gospel that stressed the holiness of God as leading to the recognition of unrighteousness in one's life and thus to the opening of the heart in repentance and faith. It is because God is holy that repentance for sin is necessary.

In Saint Paul's words to the Athenians God "commands all men everywhere to repent" (Acts 17:30). *Repentance* means to have a change of mind, and we can only conclude that in His correspondence with the churches of Asia Minor Jesus was inviting Christians who had been caught up in an attempt to prove that the church really wasn't too much different from their former world to change their minds. Walter Brueggemann catches the stance so well:

> The task of prophetic ministry is to evoke an alternative community that knows it is about different things in different ways.[6]

Yes, that's it! We are about different things in different ways. The emerging church needed to know that. We do, too. The gospel has not changed. Methods, systems, programs, and religious emotion will burn up before a God who says, "Be holy, for I am Holy" (1 Pet. 1:16). If the call to the church in the survival age of the first century was a

[6]Walter Brueggemann, *The Prophetic Imagination* (Philadelphia: Fortress, 1978) p. 6.

call to repentance for trusting in something other than Jesus alone, we cannot dare to believe He will not again call His church to repentance in a twentieth-century age of survival, which also clings to a faith in something other than Jesus.

Substituting the gospel of affirmation and experiences for one of repentance and faith is simply to offer in the name of Christ a set of words and experiences said to be better than those found in whatever culture we happen to be. Such a Christian humanism presents us only with a predator who comes as an angel of light.

Come with me on a journey back to the authentic apostolic faith when in the next chapter we examine the situation in which those first-century Christians lived. We shall then be in a better position, in the concluding chapters, to face up to some questions that could affect our churches and ourselves.

Chapter 2

WAR IN HEAVEN:
A Look at Asia Minor
Then and Now

Charlie loved his girlfriend Susan very deeply. The trouble
was simple enough. He just could not bring himself to *tell*
her. They sat in the park one day and, amid the deafening
silence of their own noncommunication, listened to the
birds.

Charlie seized his chance. "Do you know what the birds
are saying?" he asked Susan. She had no idea. "He is saying
to her, 'I love you, I love you, I love you.'"

Then awkward silence reigned again, those long silences
to which Susan had become acquainted in their friendship.
A thought flashed across her mind as the birds began to
sing again. "Do you know what they are saying now?" she
asked. Charlie could think of nothing. In exasperation she
blurted out, "'Tell me! Tell me! Tell me!'"

If Jesus loved the church, which found itself struggling
through those difficult days of the first century, was there
no way He could communicate that love? The long silence
was exasperating to the point of destroying the relationship
between Christians, and even to decaying faith altogether.
Could Jesus not speak? Could He not tell them He loved
them? Could He perhaps show it by reducing the power of
the enemy? Maybe their minister could, like the birds in
our story, convey the message for Him. Had they read
more closely a previous pastoral letter from John, their exasperation and questioning might not have been so painful.

SAINT JOHN: THE MAN AND HIS TIMES

Patmos is a rugged little mountainous island just off the coast of Turkey. It was from there, where he was living in exile, that John wrote the book of Revelation, a chronicle of some visions he had received, presumably as he kept a time of worship, for he introduced the chronicles by saying, "I was in the Spirit on the Lord's Day, and I heard behind me a loud voice, as of a trumpet" (Rev. 1:10).

About five years prior to that occasion, while he was still on the mainland, he had written a pastoral letter to the Christians at Ephesus, which in all probability would be passed around to all the churches in the area. It was a letter about God's love for His people, and it called for love to be shown among Christians in "both word and deed." The New Testament calls that letter the First Epistle of John.

In it the apostle explained his observations concerning the Person of Jesus Christ after three years of being close to Him. John, after all, was with Jesus both in times of great pressure and when he was greatly admired. He saw Christ accepted and rejected, weary and relaxed. This is what John had to say fifty years later:

That which was from the beginning, which we have heard, which we have seen with our eyes, which we have looked upon, and our hands have handled, concerning the Word of life—the life was manifested, and we have seen, and bear witness, and declare to you that eternal life which was with the Father and was manifested to us—that which we have seen and heard we declare to you, that you also may have fellowship with us; and truly our fellowship is with the Father and with His Son Jesus Christ. And these things we write to you that your joy may be full (1 John 1:1–4).

34

"We have heard, seen, and handled Jesus in all kinds of situations," John was saying, "and have come to the conclusion that in Him is eternal life. We preach Him to you that you may have communion and fellowship with us." He went on to apply the point: "Beloved, if God so loved us, we also ought to love one another" (1 John 4:11).

Do you want to hear God telling you He loves you? Then listen to each other. Care for each other. Love each other. Why are those passages so important? Because they told those early Christians that God did not only talk love; He showed it! He did not come to bring a new philosophy but a new life in a relationship of love. He is not in the business of answering only the questions of religious professionals, but rather proclaims forgiveness of sin and fellowship with God for any who believe and follow Him.

John again showed the way of God's love when he told members of the church that "whatever is born of God overcomes the world. And this is the victory that has overcome the world—our faith" (1 John 5:4). To be sure, there were those who *had* heard God say, "I love you," and in faith trusted that word. They would not accommodate to the culture, but would live as God's loved people, secure in the knowledge that in Jesus is the Word of life. There were those who, exasperated at annoying silences, would challenge God to say "I love you" on their terms.

John's letters had been written to encourage believers for a time of persecution. They contain encouragement and guidance for the reader and are quite definitive in dividing humanity in two. "He who has the Son has life; he who does not have the Son of God does not have life" (1 John 5:12). Here is the beginning of knowing the love of Jesus Christ. The silences make no difference at all. It is knowledge of His love that will keep one protected in time of difficulty.

35

Whether everyone had read John's letter or not is something we shall never know, but of one thing we can be certain. Five years later the Christians in Ephesus, and indeed in the whole of the Roman province of Asia Minor, had good reasons to cry out against the apparent silence of God's love, "Tell me! Tell me! Tell me!" Persecution broke out in a massive way. Christians had had every reason to question God's love and to ask, "Why does a God of love allow such suffering?"

The suffering in which many found themselves was very perplexing. It was all well and good for John to talk about the "victory of faith," but many Christians were watching their children starve to death as a result of parental "Christian principles." They saw members of their own family abused, imprisoned, unemployed, and often murdered because they would not abandon their faith or join in the pagan festivities and "civilized society" of their day with all its sin and injustice. John's "victory of faith" had no power, it seemed, in the great Roman oppression that was their experience.

There they were, second- and third-generation Christians, many of them having journeyed to faith in Jesus from the crucible of suffering itself, many won to Christ by the evident zeal of Christians in their love for one another, and not a few having owned their faith through the witness of Christian parents. But they were now finding that discipleship was a costly and painful process far removed from the inspiring faith that had come with great fervor to the provincial cities of the Meanda and Lycus valleys in those early days.

THE CHURCH AT THE END OF THE FIRST CENTURY

The time was approximately A.D. 96. Domitian had succeeded to the throne of an empire that ruled with great
power and authority everywhere in the world. He was an
efficient and strong ruler and, as often was the case with
such rulers, would not permit anything to threaten stability
in the empire. The emperor was worshiped as a god, and all
Roman towns erected special temples for the purpose of
worshiping him. This was not as exclusive as might at first
appear. The genius of Rome was in its readiness to recognize ethnic and minority considerations. Since it had conquered so many different countries, it was evident that a
wide variety of religions and ways of worshiping would be
taking place. The genius was to allow that to continue, but
also to require at some point each week that the temple of
the emperor be visited and, along with one's own gods, be
offered a libation. This took the form of sprinkling incense
into a fire burning on the stone altar and declaring that
"Caesar is lord." The temple housed at least one sculpture
of the reigning emperor, and often a stone frieze around the
walls depicted his great triumphs in battle and at the Senate in Rome.

The Jews, considered by the Romans to be perhaps their
most difficult international acquisition, were not generally
pressed to practice emperor worship. The Christians, who
affirmed their faith in a simple and profound creed, "Jesus
is Lord," could not obey emperor worship.

The Christians were in a different situation from the
Jews. Israel, or Palestine as the Romans called it, had nego-
tiated as a matter of international treaty, protection of Juda-

ism and freedom for Jews to worship in the ancient rites of their ancestors.

Christians were not so easily respected. They were misunderstood because, having appeared to come out of the Jewish tradition, they were simply assumed to be renegade Jews. As the faith spread it was perceived to be disloyalty to the emperor and all the glory of Rome. The empire felt threatened. Domitian had good precedence for persecuting Christians; his predecessors had also seen them to be the cause of trouble and disunity in the cities and had dealt with the problem by punishment.

Henry Bettenson has collected some early writings concerning the "punishment" of Christians. In one of these, Suetonius, an early historian who lived from A.D. 75–160, records, "Since the Jews were continuously making disturbances at the instigation of Chrestus, he [Claudius the Emperor] expelled them from Rome" (Vita Claudii 25:4).[1]

Chrestus is probably a Romanization of the Greek name, Christ, and the "disturbances" may refer to quarrels between Jews and Christians. Acts 18:2 possibly refers to this when it records Paul's visit to Corinth: "And he [Paul] found a certain Jew named Aquila, born in Pontus, who had recently come from Italy with his wife Priscilla (because Claudius had commanded all the Jews to depart from Rome); and he came to them."

Quite a colony of Jews, many of them Christians, settled in Corinth and Paul was able to stay with Aquila and minister there for two years while working at a trade of tent making. Such colonies were to be found everywhere in the provinces. Christians traveling to a new life, wanting the protection and economic security of the larger Roman cities, crossed from Italy and came to Ephesus. Many moved

[1]Bettenson, *Documents of the Christian Church*, p. 2.

further into Asia Minor to settle at one of the many small towns on the trade routes.

The book of the Revelation deals explicitly with Christians and their descendants who had left the heat of being near the center of things in Rome itself, or in Israel (which also was under Roman occupation and was so small that no one felt safe). Domitian feared the trouble Christians in the colonies might cause, just as Claudius had found himself dealing with the Jewish/Christian issue, so he was ready to react against what he perceived as dissenters. He had many informants, and a direct line called the Appian Way took the news right to his room in the Senate.

Another precedent for persecution was his famous anti-Christian predecessor Nero. The historian Tacitus records his opinion of the burning of Rome in the summer of A.D. 64:

> But all the endeavors of men, all the emperor's largesse and the propitiations of the gods, did not suffice to allay the scandal or banish the belief that the fire had been ordered. And so, to get rid of this rumor, Nero set up as the culprits and punished with the utmost refinement a class hated for their abominations, who are commonly called Christians (*Anales*, 15:44).[2]

The "abominations" probably refer to accusations that the Christians were a private society who practiced infanticide (baptism?), cannibalism (Holy Communion?), incest ("fathers, love your children"). Athenagorus, the Christian philosopher, was to complain that "three things are alleged against us: Atheism, Thyestian feasts, Oedipodean intercourse."[3] Listing the many abuses in Nero's reign, among

[2]Ibid., p. 1.
[3]Ibid., p. 2.

them that cooked food in taverns was forbidden, Suetonius added, "Punishment was inflicted on the Christians, a set of men adhering to a novel and mischievous superstition" (*Vita Neronis* 16).[4]

The Christians were far from being a moral majority, and Domitian was a sufficiently strong emperor to recognize that "abominations" or "Jewish/Christian conflict" could disturb the peace in the provinces and unity in the whole empire. Since Christians were scattered widely through the Roman Empire he would have to act swiftly and firmly against any supposed insurrection and deal efficiently with the trouble spots. His predecessors had already laid down the path he must take. It was to be "punishment with the utmost refinement," just as Nero had done twenty-five years before.

It was to the provinces that John came with Mary, the mother of Jesus. He came to the busy cosmopolitan metropolis of Asia, to Ephesus, where the one who would become the last living link with the ascended Lord would pastor a fledgling church. Here was the city to which Saint Paul and Timothy had come boldly preaching Christ to the Gentiles and adding a new dimension, a new witness, in the church. They had brought to Ephesus days that were long to be remembered.

The immense silver trade surrounding and exploiting the orgiastic worship of the fertility goddess, Diana (known as Artemis to the Greeks), was never quite the same following Saint Paul's astounding mission there. His presence produced times of growth in the Christian church. From the start Christians met in homes that nestled closely in the cities that traversed the great trade routes of Asia Minor, and the gospel of God's love spread quickly from place to

[4]Ibid., p. 2.

place. It was gossiped in the taverns; argued about in the market place; discussed and prayed about in small groups huddled around the kitchen table.

The caravans brought other Christians and contacts were made, fellowship shared, and greetings exchanged from church to church. That is how information about needs, news about ministry, and personal introductions were carried. Those believers, like us, looked for the day when Jesus would return again in power and might to conquer Satan and all his allies (the state was often viewed by Christians as a "servant of lawlessness and Satan"), to establish a reign that would outpower, outglory, outsplendor Rome. It was a commonly held hope and prayer in the church. It was great encouragement in those bad days.

To those who lived in the persecuting terror of A.D. 96, Christ's return seemed imminent. Oppression and evil multiplied; corruption flourished. Emperor worship rivaled pagan rituals in the numbers of those who took part, and was slowly becoming more debased. It was clear that Paul's letters to Timothy, to the Christians at Ephesus, to those at Colossae and elsewhere, had been right in their warnings. From his observations and assessments of what was happening among the civil authorities and in the religious sector, Paul predicted that life for the Christian was going to be harsh, misunderstood and, at the very least, complex.

But victory was imminent! It might sometimes seem slow in coming, but come it would. Paul preached hope. There would need to be endurance (see Rom. 5:3–4), but "hope does not disappoint, because the love of God has been poured out in our hearts by the Holy Spirit who was given to us" (Rom. 5:5).

HANGING BY A THREAD

The majority of Christians in those seven churches of Asia Minor were ordinary people with no more than ordinary faith. Ten, twenty, thirty, forty, and for some, fifty years had gone by since their belief and baptism. Oppressions were growing; the misunderstandings were more frequent; the persecution, more evident. There was still faith, growth, and firm expectations, to be sure. But nothing had happened to relieve the awful nagging pressure from the enemy, which first began in unnoticeable ways but was now rising to a crescendo.

Were they to conclude that they had been mistaken about Jesus? Was Christianity a fine religion, a noble ideal set among debased religion, but totally out of touch with real life? Must those second- and third-generation Christians now concede that Christianity was a good experience but, faced with the culture of the day, simply a terrible delusion which must be shattered on the hard rocks of political and social realities? Or was there a way out?

Perhaps it would be better to reinterpret the gospel so that it reflected the times in which they were living. By changing things here and there Christianity could find greater acceptability in the culture in which they seemed now to be inescapably immersed. Holding closely to the faith of the early apostles, many had been harassed, oppressed, persecuted, and killed. A great number were refused opportunity to work, some were incarcerated in jails and left to rot. At least one was reputed to have been fried alive in a huge brass bowl. And even their living link with Jesus, John himself, had been exiled, at a great old age, to a small, bleak, lonely island in the Aegean Sea. Where was the real power now?

Their life was hanging by a thread. Christians were perplexed. If oppression under the emperor Domitian created external pressure, new theology threatened to create internal decay. It seemed that the Devil himself was in control of both the world and the church. And nobody seemed to care.

WAR IN HEAVEN

From his exile home, the elderly bishop wrote to the churches in his care to share some visions given to him by Jesus. The visions concerned seven particular churches (though there were apparently many more in the area) and they were to be given in the context of encouragement. John was to convey them in the sure knowledge that God was in control, and he was to remind the Christians, "Behold, He is coming . . . and every eye will see Him" (Rev. 1:7). This was food for the hungry. It was strength for the weak.

John wrote with great confidence, in language reminiscent of the apocalyptic writings of the Old Testament (see Dan. 7), assuring Christians that God had not abandoned them. Jesus was alive and moving among the churches. But if He was moving among His churches, then He was also observing some things that were harming the Christian community and the gospel the churches were preaching.

Much of the book of Revelation is written in what I call "divine shorthand." Without doubt many first-century readers would see here clear references to the emperor (the Devil, the lawless one), though many others would accept references to the Devil at face value, and both views would extract renewed strength in the knowledge that their faith was not in vain after all. John's was a message of comfort and challenge.

He wrote in chapter 12, "And war broke out in heaven . . ." (Rev. 12:7). Our ideas of heaven, whatever their range, do not usually encompass *war*! It is with stark simplicity and shocking seriousness that John wrote about the war in heaven. He was simply explaining the background to their dilemma.

What had been happening to them at the hands of both emperor and false teaching *was* devilish. But Jesus had won the war in heaven. He is the conqueror, affirmed John, and what was happening might be likened to the swishing of the Devil's tail (the dragon in dying throes), and though it might hurt one, or even knock one over, it could not totally destroy one. That is the essence of the story in Revelation 12. The powerful word to its readers is in verse 11: "'And they overcame him by the blood of the Lamb and by the word of their testimony, and they did not love their lives to the death.'"

Certainly trouble was present. Certainly the state was persecuting. So were the citizens, the neighbors, the insipid call of pagan religion, the seductive whispers telling Christians to "cool down; don't be too conspicuous." Would they love their lives or would they die as martyrs of the faith? Would they dissolve into the background or challenge the times in which they lived? Would they be enculturated, or radically opposed to the culture?

Walter Brueggemann has tackled this issue by examining the escape of the Israelites from bondage in Egypt. Seeing Pharaoh's Egypt as a "royal consciousness" in which nothing may be questioned since the system is one which works, and has always worked *this* way, Brueggemann presents Moses as

not freeing a little band of slaves as an escape from the empire, though that is important enough, especially if you happen to be in that little band. Rather, his work is nothing less than an assault on the consciousness of the empire, aimed at nothing less than the dismantling of the empire both in its social practices and its mythic pretensions.[5]

Whether they realized it or not, the early church was in a similar business. It also was bringing to expression its deep resentment to the whole Roman system. With the seven cities as examples, the elder apostle's writings also show us today how the Devil attacks God's people. We, too, are in the business of dismantling the "royal consciousness," which has told itself and everyone else that it alone knows what is good and right for the people. But we, like John's churches, cannot attempt to dismantle, or offer alternative community, if we ourselves are part of that royal consciousness.

A gospel that is based on excitement, better times, a nicer lifestyle, even if the cross is mentioned, is in fact "cross free." It asks nothing of the receiver. It lays down no "radical alternative to the royal consciousness" by which humankind is ruled. That was the challenge John threw out to his people in the first three chapters of Revelation and throughout the rest of the book. But he also demonstrated how God would vindicate His people, and how His love would be demonstrated in the world. Finally, he showed how the war in heaven has won victory for all people, for all time, and so the book ends in triumph for Jesus and all those who follow Him to the end: "Behold, I am coming quickly, and My reward is with Me, to give to everyone according to his work" (Rev. 22:12).

[5]Brueggemann, *The Prophetic Imagination*, p. 19.

THE DIVINE CROSSWORD

The book of Revelation is certainly a word from God that has significance in every age. Some people, tragically, never get any further than a strange fascination for discovering in it a divine crossword puzzle intended to unlock the secrets of the future. They pursue a supposedly hidden agenda and find in the book clues about our two world wars, or warnings concerning the European Common Market. Any and every new confrontation in the Middle East sparks new curiosity to rethink the message of Revelation. People see almost anything that happens on the international scene as having its root in this fascinating book.

It is not my intention to follow that course of investigation. Rather, I want to examine the primary purpose of the letters in chapters 2 and 3 as they came to Christians in the first century—to believers faced with particular issues and problems of their age. Some of their issues have re-emerged as our issues also and I wish to ask the question, "Have we, the twentieth-century Christian church, anything to learn from the first-century Christians in the Roman Province of Asia Minor?"

The seven places to which John wrote were real places. You can visit them today and walk the streets of at least five of them. In Thyatira and Philadelphia nothing but fourth-century artifacts are visible. Though now no longer what they were, they once formed a circular trade route along two rivers. There is no question that Paul's letters traveled this route, which became a main conduit for the spreading of the Christian gospel. Good roads, a common language, and comparative safety enabled the word to spread through travelers, merchants, converted vagabonds, slaves, and family migration throughout the empire.

Like the medieval carpenters, whose work was recognized by the trademark they carved into the woodwork (a face, a mouse, or a sheaf of corn), John evidenced his knowledge of each city with a motif. Isolating some geographical or historical feature, he used it as a theme for the lesson being told in each message.

To those Christians who are faced with the raw excesses of a persecuting society, comes a final revelation of the Lord of the church. It is not an empty grave, or an absent-because-ascended Lord we meet, though they are valid expressions for the climax of the gospel story. Here it is a Lord of power and might who is alive and present, moving among the churches. "What this book predicts is not the product of human fancy, prone to error, but the Revelation of the mind of God concerning the church in history."[6] Jesus moved not only among the churches of the first century; He moves among them today.

Let us begin our journey, then, with the church in which John himself was overseer and with which he appears to have had the most to do. On to Ephesus!

[6]William Hendriksen, *More Than Conquerors* (Grand Rapids: Baker, 1964) p. 7.

Chapter 3

THE SECRET OF LOVING GOD:
Restoring Worship in Ephesus

"To the angel of the church of Ephesus write, 'These things says He who holds the seven stars in His right hand, who walks, in the midst of the seven golden lampstands: "I know your works, your labor, your patience, and that you cannot bear those who are evil. And you have tested those who say they are apostles and are not, and have found them liars; and you have persevered and have patience, and have labored for My name's sake and have not become weary. Nevertheless I have this against you, that you have left your first love. Remember therefore from where you have fallen; repent and do the first works, or else I will come to you quickly and remove your lampstand from its place—unless you repent. But this you have, that you hate the deeds of the Nicolaitans, which I also hate. He who has an ear, let him hear what the Spirit says to the churches. To him who overcomes I will give to eat from the tree of life, which is in the midst of the Paradise of God"'" (Rev. 2:1–7).

The rumbling grew louder and louder until one could distinguish the babble of voices—shouting, laughing, calling across the street in high-pitched excitement. The quickening pace of feet indicated that tourists were coming, and soon the shouting and laughing would turn into fevered discussion as visitors and local shopkeepers bartered over the price of a silver medallion or a silk dress. The shoppers visited around the marketplace looking for a good deal, only to make a sheepish reappearance at the first stall and accept the original offer. In the marketplace there were not only many silver merchants from whom to choose a gift, but also shops for spices, silks, herbs, pottery, and a host of exotic merchandise that had come from all over the world in one of the many ships anchored in the bay.

The visitors made their way from the marketplace toward where Harbour Street met Marble Street, where the great theater dominated the town. Marble Street was so called because it was laid with marble-covered slabs, so perfectly formed that even today a piece of paper cannot be slid between stone and the marble which overlays it.

VANITY FAIR

This was Ephesus, a bustling, jostling, bartering, busy, religious crossroad of the empire. It claimed for itself the regal title "Supreme Metropolis of Asia," being permitted by Rome to rule its own civic affairs through a democratically elected council called the "Boule." Ephesus was a very sophisticated place, indeed, boasting a fine debating center, the "Hall of Tyrannus," and a fantastic three-story Library of Celcus, with its ornately carved frontage and elegant wide steps sweeping down to a large open square beautifully inlaid with colored patterns of marble.

The theologian H. H. Farrar suggests that Revelation 18 contains a perfect description of Ephesus as "the ancient world's vanity fair" with its "'merchandise of gold and silver, precious stones and pearls, fine linen and purple, silk and scarlet, every kind of citron wood, every kind of object of ivory, every kind of object of most precious wood, bronze, iron, and marble'" (Rev. 18:12). It certainly was a magnificent place of prosperity and culture.

The visitors took a right turn at the great theater and were walking up the steady slopes of Marble Street. They stopped and cast knowing glances to each other as they spotted a footprint etched in the sidewalk. It pointed the way to the temple of Diana, the patron goddess of the city. At the temple, there were numerous priestesses ready to provide sexual favors as a tribute to love and peace and, it is said, local wives readily offered a year's free service in the worship of the fertility goddess. In the marketplace, a very lucrative business in silver charms and bracelets had grown up around the cult.

There was religious ritual, of course, and the treasury at the temple supported a bountiful welfare system for the poor and needy in the city. No traveler need go hungry, or local family struggle unnecessarily through hard times, because the temple, one of the seven wonders of the world, by the way, would come to the aid of the needy. It could be argued that *some* good came out of this particular fraternity of ancient paganism and, therefore, the ends justified the means. If it was so kind and supportive in its works, then what it stood for could not be all *bad*, surely?

Ephesus abounded in places of worship, but Diana claimed the largest following, as one might expect of the "great goddess Diana . . . which fell down from Zeus" (Acts 19:35). It was commonly held that she had fallen out of the sky in order that Ephesus, specially chosen by Zeus, the god of gods, might be her guardian.

We are forced to ask how Christians fared in that cosmopolitan society where success, prestige, and outward appearances must have held top priority. In a highly religious city filled with all manner of temples and worship possibilities, what effect did the activity there have upon the Christian community?

In A.D. 95, when Saint John was the leader of the community, they were forty years on from the time when Saint Paul had visited Ephesus, and a powerful mission had taken place. Paul, you remember, had had to make a hurried retreat as thirty thousand men filled the theater in a protest rally. The gospel Paul preached, and which many followed, had created a severe crisis in the silver industry. People were leaving the temple of Diana to worship the one true God, and consequently the sale of the silver Diana charm bracelets, and paraphernalia of the occult attached to it, had fallen away significantly. Their protest chant, "Great is Diana of the Ephesians!" (Acts 19:28, 34) echoed around the city; and at one time it seemed a riot might take place. Paul was escorted away by the Ephesian Christians, and in his heart he cherished their faith and care (see Acts 19—20).

One has only to read his letter to the Ephesians to recognize his feelings for the Christian church there. Even in that relationship, however, forty years prior to John's ministry, there are clues of what the church would later face.

PAUL IN EPHESUS

Sometime after his mission in Ephesus, Paul found himself a prisoner at the hands of Rome. As such, he was a traveler to the city because he had appealed to his right as a Roman citizen for his case to be heard before the emperor. It was a happy coincidence that brought him by way of Ephesus again. He could not come to the city itself, but the prison party having called in at Miletus gave Paul opportunity to invite the Ephesian elders to meet with him. He seems to have had two purposes in mind. The first intention was to defend his ministry among them as one in which he had been "serving the Lord with all humility, with many tears and trials . . . and how I kept back nothing that was helpful" (Acts 20:19–20). It had been an honest ministry.

His second intention was to warn against a future direction he thought some strong people in the congregation might take, leading others with them. The early church was subject, it appears, to three main problem areas: persecution, which we have already noted; internal strife, which we have mentioned and will examine again in this book; and, the most insidious problem by far, heresy.

> There was plenty of temptation to depart from "the faith once delivered to the saints." Already in Paul's time there had been an attempt to introduce a heavenly hierarchy alongside Jesus at Colossae (Col. 2:18). Pressures from a Judaistic legalism were felt in many places (see Galatians). . . . More serious was the heresy which the old Apostle John had to face, which led people to deny that Jesus was a real human being (1 John 2:22, 4:1–6).[1]

Paul had been through the white heat of controversy in so many issues of heresy and could spot the leaders equally as well as the heresy itself.

It was a severe warning Paul had to share with his elders that day, and the sad farewell, mingled with many tears, reflected that already the church was cognizant of the facts. Perhaps they had begun to experience the truth of Paul's statement, "I know this, that after my departure savage wolves will come among you, not sparing the flock. Also from among yourselves men will rise up, speaking perverse things, to draw away the disciples after themselves" (Acts 20:29–30).

Was Paul referring to the eldership itself? Was he saying that some elders would become power conscious and, in order to attract a following, would preach a gospel of easy grace? No wonder he added in his farewell to the elders, "I

[1]M. A. Smith, *From Christ to Constantine* (Downers Grove: Inter-Varsity, 1971) p. 27.

commend you to God and to the word of His grace" (Acts 20:32), for he was only too well aware that they would need to lean hard upon "the word of His grace" in the days that lay ahead.

Paul also revealed his astute mind and spiritual perception when he wrote to the young minister Timothy, whom he himself had trained: ". . . remain in Ephesus that you may charge some that they teach no other doctrine" (1 Tim. 1:3). It turned out to have been words on deaf ears for some, because of the gullibility of members who loved to follow the "men who speak perverse things." Paul described them as "always learning and never able to come to a knowledge of the truth" (2 Tim. 3:7). Paul was ever conscious of the problem of heresy, not only for the church of his own day, but also for the church that was to follow it.

The seeds of heresy sown in Paul's day might be regarded by some as simply a theological gale of meaningless, technical, and possibly even deceitful words. Forty years later that theological gale would become a whirlwind, uprooting and destroying lives, churches, faith, and ministry. Saint John would have to deal with the nominal though very vocal faith of some people who had "new theologies and practical, quick answers to life's problems" who would, like a pack of savage wolves, ravage the flock.

Paul, in Acts 20, instructed the Ephesian elders to defend and care for God's people by declaring the whole counsel of God. They were instructed to teach the Christian faith so that its followers would be strong, aware of what religious opposition looked like, and ready for the day of trouble from both church and state. What we see taking place in Revelation 2 is a record of how they simply closed ranks and tried to do their best to be Christians in the situation.

THE EPHESIAN CHURCH IN A.D. 95

It hardly need be further spelled out that the Christians to whom Saint John wrote found themselves under many great trials. Not only were they face to face with the ordinary pressures of living in a commercial, prestigious, and pagan city, they also were particularly called upon to defend the faith and maintain Christian unity against plausible but false teachings from within the church. Though Saint Paul was now dead, his letter still gave them guidance about ministry; "Be strong in the Lord and in the power of His might" (Eph. 6:10).

Their present pastor issued a similar warning: "Beloved, do not believe every spirit, but test the spirits, whether they are of God; because many false prophets have gone out into the world" (1 John 4:1). It was the desire to be strong in the Lord and to search out false prophets (teachers who craved followings and rearranged the faith in order to get them) that led the Ephesian church into a course of action that resulted in losing their "first love" (Rev. 2:4).

EPHESUS REVISITED

Biblical record, archeological research, and ancient literature conspire to give an almost complete reconstruction of life in Ephesus in the first two centuries. Walking through the site of the ancient city today is an awesome experience. Archeologists have unearthed original stones and begun to rebuild the many temples, the hospital, the odeon (where "burlesque" took place), the magnificent library of Celcus, the little houses huddled together, the upper and lower marketplaces, and, not least, the enormous, even breathtaking, main theater with its three-tiered stage and underground dressing rooms.

The marble streets, just as Paul and John knew them, give the visitor who knows it a sensation of "living the story." The houses clustered together on the hillside lend credence to the biblical picture of a close-knit community in which "all who believed were together and had all things in common, and sold their possessions and goods, and divided among all, as anyone had need" (Acts 2:44–45). Of course, this network of housing was also the dwelling place of many non-Christians who became informants to the Roman authorities.

Life was far from easy in spite of the rich communal experience of the Christian faith. On almost every public piece of sculpture and every major gateway was to be seen a relief of the Roman soldier in full armor (see Eph. 6, where Paul used this to advantage), and at every turn other reminders in stone abound, which tell the story of the grandeur, architectural expertise, civic pride, and power in which this city exulted. *This* was Rome at its best.

The Christians centered their life upon and gained strength from meeting together for worship. It is not without significance that John wrote of seeing visions on a "Lord's Day" (Rev. 1:10), at a time when the Christian community on the mainland might themselves have been meeting for worship. Any communication from Saint John would be read to the gathered community of faith at such a time.

The communication begins with realistic encouragement: "I know your works, your labor, your patience, and that you cannot bear those who are evil" (Rev. 2:2). The church in Ephesus appears to have endured well. She would be greatly encouraged to hear that the Savior knew what they had been doing. Hers had been a ministry that

Jesus described as costing much in labor and patience as they dealt with a popular heresy that consumed their time and energy on the one hand and tried their patience on the other. Having recognized false doctrine, they set their minds to root it out. It was a costly battle, which took them into a situation they had not planned, and which left them weary and worn.

THE MAJOR PROBLEM

The major problem was a teaching called the Nicolaitan heresy. Although there is debate concerning the exact identification of the Nicolaitans, there is general agreement about the teaching. It abused the truth of Christian liberty by appealing to the grace of God to justify libertine behavior. It redirected Paul's claim that "where sin abounded, grace abounded much more" (Rom. 5:20) to say, "the more you sin, the more grace there is to put it right." Or, in present-day terms, "Don't worry about doing wrong, for surely God's grace will cover you."

That was a very handy doctrine, especially in Ephesus!

The leaders of the early church knew of the Nicolaitans and their indulgence in vice, adultery, eating food offered to idols, and their love of carnal pleasure. The Nicolaitans were totally immersed in the culture of Ephesus and justified it on the grounds that they knew God and experienced His grace.

THE SEEDS OF ERROR

How did such teaching gain a hold in the church?

Recall that there were no public church buildings; the Christians met in homes all over the city and its suburbs. Saint John, the bishop and overseer of the whole Christian community, appointed elders to the different "house churches." In those small groups, those who wanted to promote their false teaching would argue their case and add to their following, even to the point of usurping the leadership.

Happily, we have evidence in Revelation 2 that the church, by labor and patience, stood against the heresy. Clearly, John's own teaching of the gospel had laid a good foundation; and it is true, both anciently and now, that when a pastor sets out to teach the whole counsel of God, a congregation can cope with most challenges it faces, both internally and externally.

How had the Christians met this challenge of carnal faith, where words were the extent and limit of Christian obedience? The English translation is almost pedestrian in describing the response as one of "labor and patience" (Rev. 2:2). We do well to search into those words in their setting if we want to catch something of the essence of the situation. The Greek word translated here as *labor* means "work to exhaustion point," and the word *patience* indicates "a persistence in being patient," or better still "a patience that persists until the job is done."

LABOR

Let us first look at this word *labor* as it is used of the Christians at Ephesus who stood against the challenge of carnal faith by "working to exhaustion point."

Have you ever watched a Christian church laboring to reach out, to worship God, to defend the faith and support its less fortunate members as it works to create a living, Christ-centered community? It has been my privilege to pastor such a church and watch Christian people support each other with prayer, thoughtfulness, repeated acts of mercy and selfless care. I have witnessed believers visiting each other with pastoral sensitivity, sharing meager possessions, giving time to listening, and healing the pains of being misunderstood, misrepresented, and even maltreated. What a joy it is to experience God's people mobilizing to serve Him, and standing against evil practices and selfishness in the community!

Seeing powerful, self-willed individuals turn to Jesus Christ and discover what it is to share pain as well as joy, to support each other in defeat as well as in victory, and to accept each other just for who they are in Christ, is a strengthening experience for any pastor. When people behave that way not once but continually, not occasionally but consistently—that is laboring for the faith to the point of exhaustion.

But laboring to create Christian community and experience its ministry did not exhaust the Christians at Ephesus nearly so much as did laboring to defend the gospel of freedom and love against those who wanted that gospel to fit their own terms. "The church has never been a place for the fashionable and dilettante," says Professor William Barclay so rightly, "but a place for those willing to sweat and work to the point of exhaustion for the community of Christ."[2] That includes defending the faith to those who would distort it or "culturally condition" it or change it, so that it fits into the age in which it is being preached.

The sadness today, as in Ephesus, could be said to be that many Christians are involved in an "undisciplined experientialism" with a "let it all happen" mentality, which itself has no root in biblical faith. If there *is* a heresy it will be relegated to that famous place which says "doctrine divides," and provided it does not challenge the "experience"

---

[2]William Barclay, *Letters to the Seven Churches* (London: SCM, 1958) p. 22.

it could conceivably survive. It never dawns on some Christians that good hard work, often "thinking work," goes hand in hand with saving faith. The Bible does not separate the two.

ENDURANCE

Jesus' second commendation to the Ephesians related to their endurance. "I know . . . your patience" is the English translation, though its meaning is much more "persistence in patient endurance," or "enduring to the end."

Endurance, when used in the New Testament, does not refer to gritting one's teeth until the dark day is finished. Rather it is to continue in the business of serving God, knowing that the dawn of a new day will surely come.

You see, the memory of Paul's disturbing mission, which had resulted in such a changed way of life there (it left the city with a depleted silver trade and a strong challenge to their own goddess Diana), still burned suspicion into the hearts of long-established Ephesian families. It was especially bothersome to those pagan families whose children, and even grandchildren, had become traitors to the cause by joining the Christian way. The Christians would need patience for that. Perhaps others, no longer convinced that Christianity need be exclusive in a moral or theological way, had propounded "freedom" in worship and faith. Again, patience would be paramount. Certainly, the Christians there lived among ever-present state persecution, and that would need patience also.

We don't know all the particulars, to be sure, but God's word is clear when it tells us that it takes persistence in patience to live with the tension caused by the presence of His Kingdom in the world. Neither can we believe that such perseverance was limited to dealing with a theological issue only. Though the text does not specifically mention it, we may safely surmise that the harassment of officialdom as it tried to make the Ephesian Christians attend emperor temples and declare that "Caesar is lord," against their own basic creed, "Jesus is Lord," played its full part. Persevering is comparatively easy when opposition is passive. In Ephesus it was far from passive.

The lessons are obvious enough and are spelled out in verse 2. Test those who, however plausibly, teach a gospel that, though using the Bible, may not be reflective of a full biblical picture. Of course, you have to spend time getting to know the Bible to do that, and the effort is often seen to be too much. Many preachers, making texts say exactly what they themselves want them to say, have become (often unintentionally) leaders of congregations who are "always learning and never able to come to the truth" (2 Tim. 3:17).

Even worse, there are pastors who teach another doctrine (in the guise of Scripture) and are like wolves who have no concern for the flock. We should test those who want to be leaders in the church, especially those who claim to be teachers because of a special calling from God, but who are unwilling to subject themselves to affirmation in the church. Interestingly enough, when affirmation does not come, such claimants to God's special revelation to be a teacher/leader in a particular church usually go elsewhere.

We are called to support each other in what really is a hostile world and we must be wary of "new insights into the traditional gospel." The Christians at Ephesus learned this well and could not be faulted on their energy and perseverance in maintaining Christian orthodoxy.

Our hearts yearn for this to be true today, do they not? Many Christian churches have sold out to image rather than truth, to methods and systems rather than faith, to Christian events rather than worship, as ways of adding excitement to their existence. They have taken on the world at its own game and find it is a dangerous sport. At the same time many of those same churches are adrift in a doctrinal storm and retreat behind the saying "Doctrine divides; liberty unites."

I have again and again come to the conclusion (in concert with fellow saints in every age!) that it is doctrine that unites, when that doctrine is biblical. It is false doctrine that divides! Can one have a Christian church devoid of doctrine? Only a heretic could subscribe to that fallacy.

THE REBUKE

With all the labor and patience against heresy and persecution in favor of Christians at Ephesus, what was it that brought rebuke from Jesus? After all, was this not a church blameless in energy and Christian orthodoxy? Were they not a community of consistent patience? Yet He said, "I have this against you, that you have left your first love" (Rev. 2:4).

There is one view that says the Ephesian Christians had been so busy defending the gospel that they had lost touch with each other and had, therefore, lost their primary commitment to each other.

Were this the case, we would not expect to see commendation for their labor and patience, for that has to be a community exercise and you need a lot of love for that. As it is, the text points to a standing *together* against false teachers and their attendant heresy.

Instead, Jesus used *love* in the New Testament sense of a divine and self-surrendering love. We are here in the realm of what the Greek text calls "love of the first kind."

REACTIVATING FIRST LOVE

Do you recognize what was taking place? They were so busy fighting for a cause, a truth, a way of life, that they had forgotten to love Jesus! In that second- and third-generation Christian church, the Lord was not dealing with Christian community relations alone but with a most deadly church killer—energy and doctrinal orthodoxy on behalf of God and His church without corporate and personal worship of the Holy Trinity.

You may be saying to yourself at this point, "What does 'first love' have to do with worship?" Everything in the world!

Worship has been defined as "loving God back." Saint John had written earlier, "We love Him because He first loved us" (1 John 4:19). Have you asked yourself, "*How* does one love God?" The question is not *should* one love God, but how should one love Him.

In the Old Testament, the first of the Ten Commandments had to do with loving God exclusively, with all one's heart, soul, mind, and strength: "You shall have no other gods before Me" (Ex. 20:3; Deut. 5:7; 6:5). The people were to worship the true God and Him alone. Further, the second Commandment dealt with graven images, *used* in worship, and the third with the Sabbath as a *day* of worship.

For Israel, then, loving God first meant worshiping Him and only Him. As one reads through the remainder of the Old Testament, so much of the story of Israel is a comparison and contrast between the times they loved and worshiped the true God and their times of apostasy when they loved and worshiped false gods.

In the New Testament, the word most often used for worship is *proskuneō*, literally, "to kiss towards." How is that for a first-class word about love! Just as human love is an act based on an attitude within a clear commitment, the same is true of spiritual love. Worship is an act of love towards God. And using this very word the Lord Jesus told the woman at the well (see John 4) that the Father seeks people who will worship Him.

Why, then, were the Ephesian Christians—or any Christians—called and chosen by God? He wanted people in Ephesus whose first order of business was to love and *worship* Him. As it was, when John sent this message, the people were still straight on the word and work of God, but they had lost their way in the worship of God. They had left their "love of the first kind."

The fresh springs of life in Jesus arise only as we worship and keep close to Him day by day, week in and week out, in the church. And what is the goal of such worship? To reach what is here described by John as the right "to eat from the tree of life" (v. 7). This is that right to be partakers of Christ in His kingdom forever.

What we need to heed in the letter to the Ephesians, then, is the Lord's warning against activities that might make us stray from that goal. We have evangelism training, social ministry training, management technique, and growth systems, all of which are valuable parts of the church's ministry to the world. But could it not be argued that we, too, like the Ephesians, have been consumed by them until we have no energy left? Might it not be argued that we often lack the worship and devotion to Father, Son, and Holy Spirit that we were saved to experience? So often our plans are just "our plans," and we can perform them with or without much reference to bowing down before Jesus, "kissing toward" the Father in heaven.

The letter to the church at Ephesus, then, brings us up sharply, and, rather like that infuriating square on the board games, sends us firmly "back to square one." Jesus did not call them to repentance for leaving Him out of their defense of the gospel. And the problem was certainly not laziness. No, He called them to repent for having lost their first love. They had replaced worship with secondary activity. In being so good at defending the faith they had discovered ways to do *only* that, and they had lost that activity of love called worship which they had known when they first came to Jesus. At that time they knew nothing else, but as life continued the freshness of a newfound faith and devotion had given way to the normality of being a non-worshiping Christian, able to survive in a hostile world.

A WORD FOR THE TWENTIETH CENTURY

The hymn writer William Cowper posed a question which I confess I need to ask constantly:

> Where is the blessedness I knew
> When first I met the Lord?
> Where is that soul-refreshing view
> Of Jesus and His Word?

It is a question we should all be asking constantly. It is time for the church at the end of the twentieth century to put aside its race to be a carbon copy of the business corporation—well activated, acceptable, and powerful enough to defend itself to the world—but without clue one about worship. There can be no substitute for devotion to Jesus now, since we shall know Him in all eternity in heavenly worship and praise. It has been said that we can only know God in direct proportion to the amount of time we spend in His presence. I suspect there is much truth in that.

It is, perhaps, not just the battle against false teachers in the church which so closely identifies today with the first-century Ephesus, but also the fact that we have learned to depend upon ourselves and discover "hidden resources of strength," therefore venerating our own progress rather than actively worshiping the Lord. It might be rightly accused, therefore, that modern evangelicalism is often strong in the Word, but weak in worship.

Perhaps the call for any age is to rediscover true worship of Jesus Christ as of first importance. We are called to rediscover His love for us and to learn to conquer evil through persevering faith in Him. We must halt excessive activity and settle down in the church as a worshiping community. We are called to rest, to be community, to be assured in the knowledge that the war in heaven is *already won*—God is God. Let Him be God. He is in control. Therefore, relax!

Certainly we are called to repent when we lose the love for Christ we had at first and begin to develop our own propensity to worship and to win this cosmic war in our own way.

Let me, therefore, encourage you to stand fast in the orthodoxy of your Christian doctrine and your service of the Lord. But never be content to stop there. To do so will produce cerebralism and busyness. Learn to keep your doctrine and duties warm—warm through the warmth of worshiping our holy God. By faith enter into the hymns, the preaching, the prayers, and the Holy Table of the Lord—whether you have great "feelings" at worship or not.

Learn to love Him back. Learn to offer Him "worthship" and praise. Never be content to stop anywhere short of true Christian worship, and as you devote yourself to the Lord in spirit and in truth you will begin to discover the whole of life is worship. You will also protect your heart from losing its first love!

Worship is the language of heaven, it is said. Enter into it now, and you will not be tongue-tied at the Gates!

Chapter 4

BE WILLING TO LOSE ALL:
The Riches of the Poor in Smyrna

"And to the angel of the church in Smyrna write, 'These things says the First and the Last, who was dead, and came to life: "I know your works, tribulation, and poverty (but you are rich); and I know the blasphemy of those who say they are Jews and are not, but are a synagogue of Satan. Do not fear any of those things which you are about to suffer. Indeed, the devil is about to throw some of you into prison, that you may be tested, and you will have tribulation ten days. Be faithful until death, and I will give you the crown of life. He who has an ear, let him hear what the Spirit says to the churches. He who overcomes shall not be hurt by the second death"'" (Rev. 2:8–11).

Pavel Timofeyvich Rytikov first entered a church to impress his drinking cronies. At twenty-two he was an experienced metal worker, brawler, gambler, and thief.

His friends, like himself, had been brought up to hate Christianity. They had read articles, for example, accusing believers of offering human sacrifices during their meetings. One day, after he and some friends had been drinking together, they decided to go to a "house of prayer" to see what the "obscurantists" and "fanatics" were up to.

"We imagined," Pavel wrote later, "that we should see some pretty horrible people, even some with horns. A chill went up our spines even as we entered the building." Pavel was so impressed by what he found that he returned again

66

and again until he finally became a believer in the Lord Jesus Christ.

In 1968, he was arrested and imprisoned for teaching children about Jesus Christ. This was Russia; and when Pavel accused the authorities of slandering believers and writing lies about them in the press, KGB Major Drokin admitted that Christians were misrepresented, but asserted that atheistic authorities had to use the "weapons of ideological struggle which are falsehood and slander."

Pavel Rytikov has spent the years since 1968 in and out of prison, and his whole family has been harassed and threatened by the Russian authorities. Between prison sentences he is not allowed to work as a pastor; and finally in 1980, for no apparent cause other than for teaching Christian faith to the children of imprisoned Christians, he was again sentenced to three years in a strict-regime labor camp in western Siberia. Keston College in England monitors his movements and last reported on him in its June, 1981, newsletter. His family continues to live in poverty.

At the same time, the politicians, professionals, athletes, and faithful atheistic "industrialists" in Russia live life on a grand scale and act as if nothing is amiss, choosing to remain totally silent against accusations from the West concerning the ill treatment of Christians in Russia. It is a guilty silence.

Christians in first-century Smyrna would identify with the persecution and poverty many Christians in Russia experience. Despite the distance in time and geography, the two places are much alike. That includes the guilty silence of the culture.

It was Plato who described every city as really two cities, the one of the rich and the one of the poor. Pliny reported that he once saw a girl married in Rome wearing a dress worth one million dollars while, at the same time, the poor in Rome were starving to death because corn, the only food they could afford to buy, was delayed in shipment from Alexandria. "The poor," said Jesus, "you have with you always" (John 12:8). Saint John wrote to his friends in Smyrna the words of Jesus to them, "I know your works, tribulation, and poverty (but you are rich)" (Rev. 2:9). Why were they poor? What did Jesus mean by this claim that they were, in fact, rich? To begin to find the answers to those questions, let us first pay a visit to the city.

THE CROWN OF SMYRNA

The hill called Pagos sweeps down to an enclosed harbor front. Nestled comfortably at the base of the hill is Izmir, a large, important, and busy city of four hundred thousand inhabitants. The harbor is an industrious international port and the waterfront, with its fashionable restaurants, expensive shops, and N.A.T.O. headquarters, reminds the visitor that this city is no second-rate place.

Further down the waterfront, local men sit outside the dimly-lit cafés, some just talking, others smoking hashish through long tubes connected to large water-filled bottles. Fresh fish is landed daily from colorful boats, recalling the ancient trade, and up to early evening it will be cooked on charcoal braziers right there on the sidewalk.

The Eastern Orthodox church keeps Christianity strongly evident here in an otherwise Islamic country.

The finest view of Izmir is from the top of the hill. It is reached by road or cable car and still called the Crown of Pagos. Here the visitor can see the definite fan shape of the city as streets and roads run down and outward like the ribs of an upturned Chinese fan; all roadways are connected at the point by the famous Golden Street, which runs parallel to the gently curving waterfront road.

At the top of the hill is one of the very few remaining sites of ancient historical note. It is the partly unearthed Roman garrison to which was brought Polycarp, bishop of Smyrna, in approximately A.D. 155 during renewed persecutions. The first martyrology records,

> . . . things happened with such speed, in less time than it takes to tell; for the mob straightway brought together timber and faggots from the workshops and baths, the Jews giving themselves zealously to the work as they liked to do. . . . they were about to nail him at the stake, when he said, "Let me be as I am. He that granted me to endure the fire will grant me also to remain at the pyre unmoved, without being secured with nails."[1]

This was sixty years after the Smyrna of John's time, of course, but it serves to illustrate the anti-Christian feeling in the city, which clearly did not dissipate with the persecutions under Domitian.

Polycarp was well known throughout the province of Asia as a Christian leader. He had been a pupil of Saint John and led the congregation at Smyrna until he was advanced in age. But the gracious old man was not allowed to die in peace. When he was at least eighty-six years old he was hunted down, pursued to a lonely farmhouse in the hills and there arrested.

The governor of Asia tried to persuade Polycarp to sacrifice to Caesar and so save himself. He would not. He was commanded to curse Christ. The reply he gave will always be seen as an impressively noble response. "I have served

[1] Bettenson, *Documents of the Christian Church*, p. 11.

Him for eighty-six years and he has never done me any wrong. How can I blaspheme my King who has saved me?" The mob, led by local Jews, rushed to gather wood for the fire, and he was burned alive.

Pagos was the Crown of Smyrna and anyone taken up there for a profession of Christian faith was well aware that it was a sure sign that death was imminent.

Today, it is a moving experience to share a Holy Communion service in the ruins of that Roman garrison and to read again words which Polycarp must surely have heard. As John's pupil he may well have been a young elder in the church of Smyrna during Domitian's persecution and would certainly have read John's letter: "Be faithful until death, and I will give you the crown of life" (Rev. 3:10). Polycarp received the crown of life in exchange for his defiant faith on the Crown of Smyrna!

AMONG THE POOR

We may be quite certain that the Christians in Smyrna, like the Christians in Russia today, were not poverty stricken by choice or by a twist of poor economic fate, but by the design of the civil authorities. If Ephesus called herself the Metropolis of Asia, then proud Smyrna, in great rivalry, described herself as the Glory of Asia. The architectural splendors of the ancient world were to be seen everywhere—in her temples, her homes, her streets, her civic buildings. On the cluttered hillside there were pagan temples to Aesculapius, the god of healing and good life; Apollo, for fame and fortune; Aphrodite, for love and peace; the opulent temple of Zeus and many, many others. What a striking contrast to the humble homes in which the Christians met to worship the King of kings.

In all the civil wars, Smyrna had chosen the right side; and when the battle honors were being handed out, Rome did not forget her loyalty. Like Ephesus, Smyrna was also made an Assize town, a center for dispensing law and order in that area of Asia Minor. This was an honor she took in her stride, since the citizens of Smyrna were already known in Rome as the proudest citizens in the whole province. They haughtily claimed Smyrna to be the finest in beauty, first to honor Caesar in worship, and the birthplace of Homer. It was a city that came to despise the unlearned, contemptuous band of innocents called Christians—those "atheists" who did not worship the great gods of all the world.

It was to the church in such a setting that Jesus described Himself as the one "who was dead, and came to life" (Rev. 2:8). Perhaps you have noticed the tense. It does not say "I am alive," which could mean that He had always been alive; but "I came to life." Christians believe that the war in heaven was won when Jesus Christ, who died on a criminal's gibbet, rose again to life and trampled down death by His own death for those who follow Him.

Unbelievers will surely point to the cross of Calvary and mock, saying "Your God is dead." They point now, as they always did, to their manmade gods, created to meet all their base and self-centered needs and proclaim that "life is fun. It all happens here. Jesus is something of the past."

Have you noticed in the text how Jesus Christ did not breathe threats to those who would slander Him and hurt His followers? To be sure, judgment is coming upon all those who do not believe in Him, but He does not now exercise power to harm those who, by rejection of Him, must yet face the sting of death. Jesus' present concern is to encourage His people in the church who for their faith suf-

71

fer pain and poverty. He does so in a way that believers in every age will understand: "Be faithful until death, and I will give you a crown of life."

The Bible tells us, and history affirms, that in the ancient world, becoming a Christian was declaring oneself an outlaw. The indications are quite clear that to claim, "Jesus is Lord," in Smyrna, where the population led the whole empire in worshiping Caesar as lord, meant putting one's life in immediate danger.

There in Smyrna, long before Polycarp's death, the church had become a place for heroes. Pavel Timofeyvich Rytikov, serving another imprisonment in Siberia while the state places his family in enforced poverty, under constant harassment, knows the pain of that heroism only too well. And the presence of Jesus, who knows our tribulation and poverty, will be as sweet to Pavel in Russia in 1984 as it was to Polycarp in Smyrna in 155, who himself had learned it sixty years earlier in a letter sent from his exiled bishop, John, to the church at Smyrna.

DEADLY POISON

Loving an enemy is easy when that enemy is on the other side of the world or has no power to harm you. For Christians under communism, our dilettante marches for personal liberties and equalities, which occupy so much of our time in the West, are a little difficult to understand. For them more important issues are at hand. They are face to face with an enemy who *does* have power to destroy them and to create untold hurt to a much wider circle of friends and family.

Christians at Smyrna were right on the scene with their enemies also. The text tells us, "Indeed, the devil is about to throw some of you into prison . . ." (Rev. 2:10). We would not be far wrong in recognizing the emperor Domitian, or more correctly his state officials in Smyrna, as the Devil in this case.

What had led to such an oppressive situation in which Christians were being thrown into prison and forced into poverty? What had they been doing to create such conditions? Perhaps, in view of the text, we would do better to ask what others had been doing to create this state of affairs. Revelation 2:9 gives us a clue when it refers to "the blasphemy of those who say they are Jews and are not, but are a synagogue of Satan."

There was in the Jewish population a strong faction of those who inherited a distrust of the Christian sect, which had itself grown out of Judaism. The way often chosen to right the wrongs (real or imagined) that our ancestors have suffered is to use slander. It would appear that this is exactly what happened here. In an orchestrated act of vengeance, and with not a few untruths I suspect, the successors of those who had lived through the Christian ministry in Paul's day and felt badly treated continued their attack on any who were Christians. In the more relaxed atmosphere of the provinces, Jews and Romans seemed to enjoy friendships that would not have been possible back in Israel. There was a marvelous opportunity for slander when the Jews repeatedly could point to the Christians' refusal to worship Caesar, here in Smyrna of all places!

Another opportunity would be at the trade guild meetings. You see, the trade guild membership was important both for finding work and for operating a business. But belonging to the trade guild also involved attending the pagan festivities of the god or goddess to whom the guild was dedicated. Jews would be very quick to point out Christians who were not attending or who made any negative comment about the guild. It was expulsion from the guild that lay at the primary root of the problem, as we shall see.

The Christians in affluent Smyrna would not allow themselves to be dominated by wealth, influence, or economic growth if that meant compromising their faith. They asked only to be permitted to live honest, quiet lives as citizens going about their business with simplicity of life.

Believe it or not, this is precisely what makes Christianity revolutionary in a world dedicated to personal fulfillment, success, and individual wealth and power. Christians, of course, are not crusading revolutionaries out to conquer the world. More particularly, we are an alternative society involved in the world to share the compassionate caring love of the Savior, but not to be governed by its unwritten rules. In the empire, where everything was settled from above, any withdrawal from the communal life of local society that appeared to challenge the status quo was considered revolutionary, and the Christians would pay dearly for having a mind governed by someone other than the emperor. The Jewish agitators would make the most of the situation.

That is where the trouble began in Smyrna. The deadly poison of slander grew into a collective voice of prejudice, smirking, laughing, and pointing at the church. The word of prejudice traveled through the business world; objections to certain rites at the trade guild meetings were noted; consistent refusal to worship at Caesar's temple was apparent.

SUFFERING

Two words almost hidden in the biblical text give us the clue to what was taking place. We shall examine them sepa-

rately. "I know your . . . *tribulation,* and . . . *poverty,*"
said Jesus.

In his book *Men Made New,* the Reverend John R. W.
Stott draws attention to Saint Paul's use of the word *suffering* (NKJV, *tribulation*) in Romans 5:3–5: ". . . we also glory
in tribulations, knowing that tribulation produces perseverance; and perseverance, character; and character,
hope. Now hope does not disappoint. . . ."

We do not enjoy suffering as a pleasure; neither do we
see it as purgative. The word translated here as "suffering"
(or "tribulation") comes from a Greek word meaning "troubles" or "pressures." Dr. Stott has demonstrated that *thlipsis* is best understood as the "pressures of a godless world."
This places Paul's "rejoicing under suffering" in an understandable context. We rejoice under the pressures of a godless world because this pressure produces endurance, the
endurance produces character, and so on.

The interesting and helpful thing for our study is this:
When Jesus spoke of the tribulations in Smyrna He did so
specifically with this word *thlipsis,* "pressures of a godless
world."

Passive Christians are often persuaded that the world is
not really such a hostile environment, but things never look
quite so bad when you are not in the battle! And passive
Christians are not usually found in the battle.

The Very Reverend Philip French-Beytagh was at one
time dean of Johannesburg Cathedral in South Africa. He
was imprisoned for a series of stands he made against apart-
heid as it related to black and white Christians worshiping
together.

During a period of solitary confinement, when the only
food he had was bread and water, he concluded one Sunday
that he should celebrate Holy Communion. He had no
books, no bread and wine, no choir, no liturgy. But what he

did possess were the words of Jesus locked in his mind where no one could get at them! Those words came to life in a new way. Bread and water replaced bread and wine, and the dean of Johannesburg Cathedral said later that the prison cell became a celebration; the words of Jesus the ultimate liturgy; the angels of heaven the choir. Right there in the prison cell, he worshiped with greater depth than he had in any magnificent cathedral.

There is great benefit in hearing and hiding in one's mind the words of Scripture, as the dean discovered. It is the greatest defense in temptation, the greatest strength in persecution, and the greatest source of inspiration. Surely the words of Scripture and the teachings of Jesus brought comfort under *thlipsis,* the pressures of a godless world.

We, too, face similar pressures in the world. The Christian sets new goals, applies new values, works in new dimensions of love that stand against the tide of a godless world. The Holy Spirit determines for us new sensitivity and ministry, which lead us to pray, work, and respond to our world. These, too, lead into conflict, for Christian ministry is seen as constituting a radical form of criticism of society.

Christianity in Smyrna appears to have been something of a challenge to both business and private sectors of the town and to have caused much embarrassment to court authorities. Consequently, the civic powers listened to the slander and probably were very much a part of it all. They acted on what they heard and on their own prejudices in such a way that the Christian population was forced into great personal suffering, many being imprisoned, and now on the verge of something even worse.

The top of the hill, the Crown of Smyrna, as we have said, housed the Roman garrison—the place of execution. In an earthly sense, all that many Christians could anticipate was that final persecution, a visit to the Crown of Smyrna—there to face death.

Most of us suffer very little for our faith. True, there is some insidious persecution present in the rejections we sometimes feel because at work, or in the neighborhood, we fail to involve ourselves in things that we know will deny Jesus. We sense the snickering of non-Christian friends when we make a stand for faith, or the mockery sometimes present when we try to share the meaning of our faith in Jesus Christ (which is why it is so hard to witness to family and friends), but on the whole we can survive and sometimes even be the victor!

In such a time let us "hide God's word in our hearts" and, like Dean French-Beytagh, have a store of spiritual material that will come to our aid whenever we find ourselves under the pressures of the godless world.

POVERTY

As if suffering in its many forms were not enough, Smyrna's faithful took a further, and often more difficult, blow for their persistent love of Christ. It came in the shape of poverty. (Many Christians in Russia can identify with this part of the message to Smyrna, also!)

The word Jesus used for poverty in this passage is not the ordinary sense of being poor, but that of "utter destitution." It is a word that suggests vagrancy. Christians in Smyrna were vagrants and homeless and not only did Jesus know it, but He described it as *being rich*! What could He mean? Why were they materially destitute? Had they decided to give up on life and form an alternative society that was to have no contact with the wicked world, and the final result had been this utter destitution?

It would be helpful for us in answering our questions to take note of three things about their poverty.

First, it is generally true that Christians in the early church tended to be, though not exclusively, from the slave class and therefore accustomed to being poor. By the end of the first century, however, and particularly in the provinces, this was less true. An increasing number of wealthy people became Christians; and there is evidence that they used their wealth, and attendant power, to minister among the Christian community. But, nonetheless, poverty was widespread.

Second, Smyrna was among the wealthiest of cities in the empire. That in itself suggests the possibility of some employment, certainly enough to avoid destitution even if it did leave one poor. It is worth noting that poverty existed side by side with this great wealth; for much has not really changed in Smyrna today apart from its new name, Izmir.

The third thing we need to notice concerning the Christians' poverty in Smyrna is this: it was particularly the *Christians* who were destitute in this wealthy city. That is surprising, for Christians have always applied themselves to work as an affirmation that they were serving God in their labors.

There is no way that God would have heaped such singular praise on a church like Smyrna if its members were so unwilling to work that they had allowed themselves to become destitute. It is biblically evident that although Jesus is always on the side of the poor, He is not to be aligned with the lazy, arrogant, work-shy destitute. There is a world of difference between the poor and the unmotivated!

BEING FAITHFUL
It was certainly a dangerous thing to be a Christian in Smyrna, just as it is in many a Communist or Muslim place today. But the Christian cannot be silent, for the manner of

life bespeaking the faith should of itself witness. The Christian will not be found in a place that dishonors the name of Jesus or spend time with people who do so. The Christian looking to live an honest and true life will avoid malpractice in business, a poor job of work, injustice, and shady practices. In every area of life, Christians working to reflect the kingdom of God will "pursue righteousness, godliness, faith, love, patience, gentleness" (1 Tim. 6:11). It was doing just this that produced such a strong reaction in the unbelievers at Smyrna and geared them into action. It was a prototype of reactions that can still take place.

One wonders if today our Christianity is even noticeable beyond a few good deeds or religious statements we make at opportune moments. Have we now become so tolerant and accommodating that belonging to a Christian church is rather like belonging to a nice (if a little pleasantly anachronistic) club, or following a good (if sometimes rather time-consuming) hobby that concerns itself with statistics, numbers, contacts, buildings, and a quaint community activity on Sunday mornings?

Has the church become so harmless, so dehumanized, so worldly that the world no longer notices us? Are we wrapped up in a folk religion in which we preach to ourselves in order to trigger predictable responses, but have nothing to say in our society about ethics, morality, honesty, marriage, family life, truth, integrity, relationships, work, and business because we ourselves are tainted in all or some of those areas? Have we reached the point where we are satisfied with a verbal assent to faith but expect no great change in a person's life?

No one could accuse the Christians at Smyrna of "spiritualized Christianity." Their radical application of the gospel challenged the city fathers until the response was to force believers onto the streets. But then, those Christians could challenge the world with "Thou shalt not steal" because their business was honest. They could preach divine purposes in the permanence of marriage because their marriages survived. They could teach, "Thou shalt have no other gods but me," because they were not sold on their own or anyone else's ego, which itself is one of the major gods of present day theologies in the world and the church.

If the church does not want to preach repentance as the first step of faith lest it "puts someone off the gospel of love" (as some preachers say), we *dare* not preach a gospel that says following Christ is costly.

POOR MAN, RICH MAN

What word of encouragement, then, could this church expect from heaven in all that was happening to them? Under the circumstances, it seemed like a strange word: "I know your works, tribulation, and poverty (but you are rich)" (Rev. 2:9). But the authority of Jesus, His power to transform, was to be found precisely in His own poverty, hunger, and grief among His people as He walked this earth. Thus however real their poverty, hunger, grief and living as non-persons, they were in fact rich. Jesus was among them! The Gospels record that He had promised to be with His people whenever they were making disciples (see Matt. 28:19–20); and now that such activity had led them into devastating destitution Jesus would not abandon the outcasts. He was present. It was not sympathy but security that Jesus had in mind; not power but promise; not a cross but a crown; "Be faithful unto death, and I will give you the crown of life," He said (v. 10).

And *there* is the key to richness in the midst of poverty. To sing and to dance, to heal and to forgive, is release to the one who is bound in spirit, whether that binding comes from poverty, oppression, or victimization. To be able to forgive is a rich possession. The Christian has been given authority to forgive by Jesus and is called to do so. "Forgive us our debts, as we forgive our debtors" (Matt. 6:12). Such freedom and release! Such immense and great riches! Such promised reward! "Be faithful unto death, and I will give you a crown of life," said Jesus.

The word *crown* could refer to a royal personage, or one who wears by right a royal crown *(diadēma)*, in which case it would be an inherited right. Alternatively, it could refer to a moment of glory when the reward is a crown *(stephanos)* to mark the victory. The word used in Revelation is this word *stephanos*. Let us look, then, at three possible usages of a crown of victory.

1. *A crown of victory*. This is the laurel wreath given to a winning athlete. Saint Paul used that idea when he said, ". . . I have finished the race. . . . Finally, there is laid up for me the crown of righteousness . . ." (2 Tim. 4:7–8).

2. *A festal crown*. This was used on holidays and special festive occasions. Often it was worn at weddings to symbolize to the couple the greatness of the day. It is still used in the Greek Orthodox wedding service.

3. *A crown of reward*. Such a crown was a public gift to honor leading statesmen as a reward for services to the community. Often their crowned image would also appear on local currency following the crowning ceremony.

The third option, in spite of Paul's frequent use of the athlete picture, is commonly agreed to be the way the word is used in Revelation 2. Given their faithfulness under persecution, the Smyrnans deserved reward rather than a crown of victory and with it much honor in the community of Christ. Rich because He was present with them, they were also rich for the reward they were soon to receive for their faithful service in God's name.

NO SECOND DEATH

Since believers will receive the reward of a crown of life, there can be no second death for them (see v. 11). What on earth can that mean? Whoever heard of a *second* death?

Many phrases and ideas of Judaism carried over into everyday phraseology and were often used to convey current ideas and idioms. Some of those were spoken in conscious religious settings and others in more proverbial connotation. It was one thing, for example, to talk about falling standards in a society with a jocular, "Well, folks, spare the rod and spoil the child!" as a personal response to the problem. It was quite another for the city fathers to sit down and discuss the proverb in terms of legislating harsh punishment for even the slightest offense based on the discipline of "spare the rod and spoil the child."

The idea of a second death is in this similar vein. It was a teaching that said one's life was tested against a physical death, which was followed by a second death, a spiritual death, depending on how well one had lived on earth. The second death was seen to be a total separation from God. On earth, one was within the scope and possibility of God's care and received His blessing according to how well the law was followed and practiced in everyday life. Physical death would place one beyond that scope, so if one had not lived as a good Jew, the second death, a spiritual death, then occurred.

Of course, all Gentiles would go that way, except perhaps "Godfearers"—Gentile converts who tried hard to be good Jews—and so would bad or law-breaking Jews.

Can you hear the Jews touting their rabbinical proverb as they saw the destitute Christians dying of starvation? Can you hear their, "Well, they are getting ready for the second death"? It would be said confidently because many of the Christians were Gentiles, and second death was all they could expect. The Christians who were Jews had not kept the law faithfully; indeed, by becoming Christians they had rejected their heritage, so the second death was inevitable.

John not only refuted the theology, but stated with great boldness what Jesus had told him to write, namely, ". . . He who overcomes shall not be hurt by the second death" (Rev. 2:11). John had written with the same confidence five years previously: "He who has the Son has life . . ." (1 John 5:12). And does not that agree with the promise, "Be faithful until death, and I will give you the crown of life"?

SMYRNA FOR OUR DAY

In this age we are obsessed with success. People will lie for it, cheat for it, put their families at risk for it, expend the lives and talents of others for it. But *have* they must. Yet "success" in our modern sense is not a biblical idea. As we understand it today, it is built on self-esteem and self-deception, however much the minister in the pulpit or the businessman might spiritualize it or argue the idea away.

It is in these very areas, it seems to me, that the letter to Smyrna challenges us today. If success and the way to it means we must "give a little, take a little," then do it we will. If it means a tortuous reinterpretation of faith, preaching a contentless gospel, or avoiding certain "sensitive" issues in our preaching, then we shall do that. If it means taking on the shade and color of the local breed so that we find maximum ease and acceptance, then that will be done—anything to ensure our success. Success is the god; we, its worshipers. Christianity should never be allowed to challenge friendships, never get in the way of personal ambitions, never interfere with a business deal, however questionable, and never be allowed to influence the ever-hungry beast of greed, with its endless appetite. At least that is what many Christians seem to imply. For them Smyrna would appear today to be a sellout.

Weakness, failure, frailty—these are words we do not like. But in weakness came strength for a church willing to believe in Jesus' words, "You are rich." There was strength in a church willing to believe that God would not abandon them. There was strength in a church which could lift its eyes beyond its weakness, destitution, hunger, tragedy, and defeat. These people did not choose poverty. But if success could only be bought for the price of a "culturally conditioned faith," Christians at Smyrna would have nothing to do with it. If having no guild membership meant no work, poverty, destitution, and death, then faithfulness to Jesus Christ and His gospel was to be the altar on which such decisions were made. All pretensions to success or personal power were second place. And that resonates with discipleship. Amy Carmichael captured the essence of that faithfulness in her poetry:

> From subtle love of softening things,
> From easy choices, weakenings,
> (Not thus are spirits fortified,
> not this way went the crucified)
> From all that dims Thy Calvary
> O Lamb of God, deliver me.

Christians at Smyrna recognized the cost of discipleship. They were able to make the journey from prosperity to poverty. They knew that God's grace was sufficient in whatever situation they might find themselves. If it was to be rejection, hardship, or even death, they would remain faithful to Jesus Christ rather than deny His name.

Exotic, warm, and beautiful, Izmir hugs the side of the hill Pagos, on which were once housed pagan temples. One beautiful moonlit evening as I stood on the waterfront and glanced upward to the Crown of Pagos, I reflected on this once vitally important Roman city and I mused.

Izmir is the only Christian city in a country given to Islam. Here, in ancient Smyrna, where the faith was outlawed, God's jewel shines as a light in the darkness. Here is to be found the descendant of a church whose faithfulness led to a crown of life. In Smyrna, A.D. 95, it looked as if Christianity was about to die with its followers; but today it flourishes, and the words of Jesus in Revelation are poignant. "To the angel of the church in Smyrna write, 'These things says the First and the Last, who was dead, and came to life.'"

The Lord's church is still alive and well in Smyrna today, a tribute to the rejected people for whom He had nothing but unqualified praise.

Chapter 5

RESISTING THE DEVIL:
Satan's Seat in Pergamos

"And to the angel of the church in Pergamos write, 'These things says He who has the sharp two-edged sword: "I know your works, and where you dwell, where Satan's throne is. And you hold fast to My name, and did not deny My faith even in the days in which Antipas was My faithful martyr, who was killed among you, where Satan dwells. But I have a few things against you, because you have there those who hold the doctrine of Balaam, who taught Balak to put a stumbling block before the children of Israel, to eat things sacrificed to idols, and to commit sexual immorality. Thus you also have those who hold the doctrine of the Nicolaitans, which thing I hate. Repent, or else I will come to you quickly and will fight against them with the sword of My mouth. He who has an ear, let him hear what the Spirit says to the churches. To him who overcomes I will give some of the hidden manna to eat. And I will give him a white stone, and on the stone a new name written which no one knows except him who receives it"'" (Rev. 2:12–17).

There is a story told in the ancient world that when Egypt stopped its supply of papyrus to Asia Minor as a political sanction, the one place expected to feel the impact more than anywhere else would be the illustrious Pergamos.

The residents there, however, were not easily disturbed by the sanction. They had enormous confidence in their men of genius, as they had every right to have, and in the many and varied skills in the trade guilds. Surely they would be able to come up with something.

THE PARCHMENT OF PERGAMOS

True to form, that's just what they did. Their reply to Egypt's embargo was to invent a method of producing extremely thin layers of animal skins, which made perfect manuscript material. They called it "Pergement," which over a period of time came to be known as parchment.

Parchment, however, is not the sole notable claim to genius in a city with such a long and noble history. Historical record and archeological digs have revealed that the city was founded seven hundred years before Christ and became one of the famous Hellenistic sites when Alexander the Great recognized its potential as a fortress. He gave Pergamos to another famous commander, Lysimachus, as a personal gift.

During the Roman period the city grew, developing into a center for healing and also a center for worship of many Greek and Roman gods, though without doubt Aesculapius, the god of healing, was a central deity.

Pergamos was built atop an extremely steep hill, with very thick walls for protection, its city gates guarded by watchtowers. It is difficult to believe a city could be built there.

Building a complex city in such a place produced many problems, not the least of which was the provision of a regular water supply. Early in her history, though, the brains of Pergamos triumphed again. Huge cisterns were created to harness rain, and feed pipes led to reservoirs in the hillside. In this way water was made available at different levels on the hill, and an aqueduct carried more water across the

Kozek plain. The city was supplied with water from above and below.

The center of the city was the Acropolis, on top of the hill, and it was a very sophisticated place, with buildings for education, worship, military guard, and athletic pursuit. There was a theater even this far up, and a gymnasium.

From this high vantage point one can see across the valley the remains of what was once a splendor in the ancient world. It is the famous healing center, which rubs shoulders with present day Bergama. The center gained its greatest following under Galen, the doctor of kings and emperors, sometime between A.D. 131 and 260.

BOGUS BELIEF

To give some practical idea of how cult worship worked and how plausible it was, it would help if we visited that place before focusing our attention on Satan's seat in Pergamos. A sacred road, common in Hellenistic times, connected the lower city to Aesculapian, and this road has now been excavated. As you walk along it, the tall columns indicate where the shops used to be on either side of the road.

This colonnade leads to a large square, which used to be the temple of Aesculapius. It was 120 feet high, and around the walls were paintings depicting the god of healing at work. Right at the center of the room, beneath a domed roof, stood one piece of furniture. It was a short, round, stone pillar standing 4 feet high and carved on the side with two intertwined snakes. The top of the stone was slightly concave and a small fire burned there continuously. This was the altar to the god Aesculapius.

Visitors were met here by a priest and obliged to buy a measure of incense, which was to be deposited upon the flames as a votive offering of trust in Aesculapius. A slave then led the patient through huge brass doors into a large park skirted about with colonnaded walks on all sides. Across the far side of this villa was the sacred pool, with priests in attendance, and the patient was taken there and invited to step down into ankle deep water.

The priest ascertained the nature of the illness and then began to determine the "votive offering" for healing. This meant bartering with the patient to find out what price was willing to be paid to appease Aesculapius and secure the healing. If it was enough, then water would flood into the pool. If it was not, only a trickle would appear. Effective healing was possible (but not guaranteed) only if the water rose to waist level. The first sum discussed was never enough! Bargaining would continue until a price was reached that was satisfactory for the god to send enough water into the pool. Unknown to the patient, a priest, hidden on the other side of the pool and listening to the process, was lifting or dropping a subterranean slab of stone that allowed a spring to feed water into the pool. The higher the price, the sooner Aesculapius sent water!

Treatment began with sessions of psychotherapy suggesting that healing was an already established fact. Once a positive-thinking attitude was established, the patient was given a sacred mud bath and then transferred to the herbal bath where a strong drug vapor was inhaled. When sufficiently sleepy from the drug effects, a long walk along the "whispering corridor" would lead to the temple of Telesphor, a round building with six large alcoves in which were already a number of sleeping patients. Some would have been there for days, heavily drugged, and the new patient would collapse into an alcove and join them, his head fuzzily aware of heavenly voices singing and pronouncing healing in the name of Aesculapius. He had been aware of those voices since he entered the underground corridor.

But what was not known was that the voices came from priests who were whispering softly down long shafts at ground level. It was a semiconscious, not unpleasant, floating experience of well-being, in which the "heavenly voices" were welcome partners. Once the drug wore off, the patients made their way back to the villa, where more positive-thinking psychotherapy took place, which might be followed by a further sacred mud treatment or convalescence at the villa. There were gardens in which to walk, a library, or debating in the philosophical hall available to the convalescent, or one could simply relax on the covered terraces.

CITY ON A HILL

The worship there in the clinic, however, was only a microcosm of the many and varied deities it was possible to worship in every area of life, from fertility to fame and from healing to occultic powers over a competitor.

At the summit of the hill on which was built the Acropolis were gods for every occasion—Dionysius, Hera, Athena, Aesculapius, Serapis, the sacred place of Demeter, and many patron gods of the trade guilds—and a very large temple in which to worship the emperor. There is a strong tradition that it was this temple Jesus had in mind when he referred to "Satan's throne." The state cult required nominal acceptance, but not fervent support. That nominal acceptance, however, was obligatory. Add to that fact also that at this time Domitian had decreed that he should be known as "Our Lord and God." That Domitian demanded to be worshiped, and given that many references to Satan in Revelation are hidden references to the emperor, there is strong support for the temple of emperor worship as the "Satan's throne" of Pergamos.

Twice in this letter Jesus encouraged the Christians by reminding them that He knew that where they dwelt was the place of Satan's throne. Given the number of pagan deities, the worship of whom masked all manner of sin and sexual immorality (religion and sexual indulgence have often formed a major alliance in both ancient and modern cult worship), it would not be surprising if the whole hill was envisaged as Satan's throne!

The pressure on Christians, however, was not simply the plausibility of pagan worship. Sir William Ramsay tells us that "Placed amid the uncongenial society of the Roman Empire the Christian church found itself necessarily in opposition to some parts of the Roman law and custom."[1]

Seeing how Christians were surrounded by so much paganism, and constantly under pressure in their refusal to worship the emperor as God, one catches something of the difficulty they faced living in Pergamos.

SATAN'S THRONE

There are other opinions about Satan's throne, for the phrase has occasioned much discussion. Some suggest that among all the pagan worship, there might have been an actual seat reserved for him in the temples. Certainly there was much occult and "black art" in paganism.

Another popular view among some Christians has been that the phrase refers to the fact that believers in Pergamos were so accustomed to sin that they had made the place a home for Satan. To take that view is less understandable than any other theory for it misses the praise on Jesus' lips for the believers who did not deny His name (see v. 13) even under such pressure. And it fails to take into account

[1]Sir William Ramsay, *The Church and the Roman Empire*, (Grand Rapids: Baker, 1979) p. 177.

the mention, also in verse 13, of the martyrdom of Antipas who died for his faith.

Not much is known about Antipas. There is a tradition that he was a bishop in the church, perhaps a leader of the congregations in Pergamos. The text speaks of his being put to death in the city, and tradition has it that he was fried alive in a huge brass bowl. Perhaps this was an occasion for occult worship by the pagan persecutors, with an offering of human sacrifice.

The temples of Asia Minor were not houses of virtue in any sense of the word. Nobody would say of them, as might be said of modern places of heresy, "Well, they're wrong, but at least they are nice people." If Antipas's fate sounds shocking, consider a common act of barbarism in the name of worship. A special prayer or message to the gods was inscribed with a sharp instrument on a child's body and the child was then thrown into the fire as human offering, the spirit of the child leaving its body to carry the message to its destination.

Remember, this was a world of abject superstition and a time when Satan was worshiped almost without the worshipers knowing it. "Satan's throne" could be identified almost anywhere—it is by no means as definitive as Sir William Ramsey suggests (and with which many agree):

> Again, the importance attached during this persecution to the worship of the Emperor, and the hatred for this special form of idolatry as the special enemy, have dictated the phrase addressed to the church of Pergamos, "Thou dwellest where the throne of Satan," i.e., the temple of Rome and Augustus, "is."[2]

[2]Ibid., p. 297.

Standing on the summit of Pergamos viewing the magnificent scene of the valley below, I came to my own conclusions about a possible identity of Satan's throne. Of all the temples and altars on Pergamos, the one that is truly most breathtaking and spectacular is a massive platform on the very edge of the summit, with a dominating view of the valley for at least twenty miles each way.

This projection is what remains of an altar, measuring 9×9 meters (or 29×29 feet) that was dedicated to Zeus, the god of gods, the savior among gods. The platform of the altar was approached by ascending steps and resembled a huge throne from which a king might survey his empire. Around the base of the altar was carved a record of the battle of the giants, a masterpiece of sculpture, that has now been removed to the British Museum.

On this huge platform animal sacrifices were burned twenty-four hours a day by a constantly changing team of priests. The sickening smell of burning animal flesh permeated the air in Pergamos, and all day long a column of smoke curled upward as a token symbol, through the sacrifices, on behalf of all the gods worshiped here. The smoke could be seen from miles around and served to keep the supremacy of Zeus ever in the public eye. It also served as a constant challenge to Christian believers that Satan was indeed at home here.

Perhaps Saint John recognized Pergamos as a place that would in turn suffer God's judgment, or perhaps it was to make a point of confidence for the Christians, that he wrote later, "He has avenged on her the blood of His servants . . . her smoke rises up forever and ever!" (Rev. 19:2–3).

The word *throne* in the phrase "where Satan's throne is" (v. 13) depicts something more than just a special seat. It speaks of power and authority over an empire. It speaks of

93

kingship in a nation. For me, the altar of Zeus fits them both perfectly, not only as a place surveying an empire, but also as significantly symbolic of power and authority, its dark splendor placing all other paganism in the shadows as it lords over the territory like a throne in the skies.

It is my view that in Pergamos, "where Satan's throne is," we have one of John's secret codes referring directly to that altar as he saw in it a blatant challenge to Christian faith and worship. The altar was not only a reminder concerning the place of Satan's authority but also a tender reminder from the Lord: "I *know* . . . where you dwell . . . where Satan dwells" (italics mine).

LIVING AND STAYING

What has all this to do with the story, as it develops, and what can Pergamos say to us today?

Just as we often feel there is no way of escape from the evil that surrounds us, the Christians in Pergamos were forced to find the Lord's way in the midst of the paganism and immorality that existed there. There was only one final escape. For when the New Testament speaks of a Christian's living in a particular place, it uses a word that means temporary accommodation. The writer to the Hebrews put it succinctly: "Here we have no continuing city, but we seek the one to come" (Heb. 13:14).

THE DWELLING PLACE

The New Testament encourages believers to live as people who will ultimately be on the road again. We are not to get too settled in the world, but to live as those who are passing through both its troubles and rewards to a better city. When Jesus chose His words to address the church at

Pergamos, therefore, we may be sure that He was doing so carefully: "I know . . . where you dwell . . . where Satan dwells."

The word He used for *dwell* is the same in both cases. It is the word used regularly in the New Testament to speak of a *permanent residence*. The Christians were placed there at Pergamos, of all places, for the rest of their lives. They were permanent residents in the place where (so it seemed) Satan had a residence. There was to be no escape until they came, through death, to their heavenly Father's home.

Jesus commended some of the believers for their stand in faith and refusal to deny His name even in that situation. God had called them to live out their life for Christ in that place, and since Christianity is not about running away, but about victory and conquest where sin rages a constant battle, they stayed as faithful witnesses to Jesus Christ.

There, where the god of healing was worshiped under the satanic emblem of snakes, objectionable as that was for the Christian believer, the church was called to gather and grow. There, where the smell of sacrifice to Zeus filled the air, and religious persecution came at the hands of a people ready to worship any god, the Holy Eucharist was offered continually. It was there, in pagan Pergamos, that Christians were described as permanent residents!

Perhaps there is a special word for us just there. In this present period of Christian history we seem to have developed a kind of caravan of Christians who suppose that their own personal fulfillment and joy is God's sole concern. There has developed in the church a theology of "needs," which presupposes that a church has only one function, and that is the fulfillment of those needs.

The Christians at Pergamos are also a challenge to us pastors who, more often than we care to admit, fulfill our own egos by searching out opportunities to prey upon other churches. We programmatically create a gathered community from Christians who are under pressure elsewhere, and then justify the resultant "Christian ghetto" by defending it as a special ministry. Write it on your heart, dear reader. God is aware of your place of residence. He knows the darker side of your locale, its frustrations, privations, and pressures. And He is not ashamed of you any more than He was of the faithful believers who lived in pagan Pergamos. And that is exactly the point of the debate about Satan's throne; not where it was or what it was, but rather that in the place where Satan lived, in Pergamos, the Christians did not deny their faith, but held fast to the Lord's name (see v. 13).

If Satan's throne highlights for us the martyr spirit in those who displayed faith in the name of Jesus, the phrase also forces into the open a faction in the church who preferred creature comforts to sacrificial living. While Jesus was careful to single out the faithful believers, He did not fail to isolate those who constituted a great danger for the church. Paganism from outside the church could be counteracted by the church. Paganism inside was another matter.

The internal cancer arose primarily because there were those for whom Christian sacrifice was a rather narrow interpretation of the gospel. Since it was easier to be friendly than faithful, they decided it would become necessary to make some adjustments in the church. The problem arose from two related (but distinctly different) doctrinal errors in the church. One error was called Nicolaitanism and the other "the teaching of Balaam." Both religious heresies are mentioned elsewhere in the letters to the seven churches of Asia Minor and were quite common in the emerging church. The errors were encouraged in the church by two sociological demands:

1. Other religions and paganism, which many Christians had so recently abandoned, under Roman pressure for tolerance looked quite plausible.

2. The sinful man-centeredness of much Christian theology looked for acceptance and popularity from others. In that way the door was open for accepting pagan practices into Christian life and worship.

Those two demands opened the door for some Christians to justify a reinterpretation of Christian behavior on the grounds that Christianity and paganism worship the same God ultimately. No doubt the healing center was justified on the basis that it was doing a good work. The internal cancer was probably a mixture of both areas, for the Nicolaitans took the gospel of freedom in Christ and made it a heresy of licentiousness, while the Balaamites said that the best way to get the gospel to unbelievers was to become like them in lifestyle. It was an unholy ecumenism in both issues.

THE BALAAMITES

To discover the full implication of the two heresies upon the church, then and now, we should examine their nature. The first group is described simply as "those who hold the doctrine of Balaam" (Rev. 2:14).

Who was Balaam? We would not go astray in connecting him to his Old Testament namesake. There he began as a good prophet of Israel, being described as a prophet who knew the difference between good and evil (see Num. 22—24). He was, however, very easily bought for the right price and persuaded ancient Israel, against its better judgment, to share in an "ecumenical project" with foreign nations (see Num. 31:16). The project led to forbidden marriages, forbidden worship, apostasy, all acts of disobedience against the Covenant relationship this people had with God Almighty. The result was a plague that killed many of the people and sent the whole nation into mourning (see Num. 25).

The way the Balaamite heresy worked in the first-century church was strikingly similar. It was effective in persuading Christians that all things religious were, by definition, basically good (though admittedly not to their way of thinking) and would eventually lead to God. Unfortunately they did not agree on the first basic, which for Christians was their creed, "Jesus is Lord."

We do well not to be too harsh in our criticism of the early church, and not to critique ourselves. The trade guilds were excellent in charitable works for their members. The healing center had much to commend it. The world was full of good, happy, law-abiding, hard-working pagans! It still is. The church was seduced by a well-meaning Balaamite movement. It still is.

THE NICOLAITANS

If the Balaamite movement was a conscious, perhaps even well-defined, executive influence in the church, the Nicolaitans consisted of individuals who changed the gospel to suit their private theology of freedom and love. Rather than being a concerted theological assault on the church, the Nicolaitans were more of a sophisticated sniper operation. They added insult to injury by describing their wicked lifestyle as "Christian liberty."

The heresy originated in a *privatized* interpretation of the gospel. Such interpretation is a natural successor to a personal decision for Jesus Christ that is made largely because of the benefits promised.

Let me unpack that statement some. If a decision for

Jesus Christ is not based totally upon repentance for sin, then there is little on which to call for a changed lifestyle. If the former lifestyle is not recognized as sin, then the purpose in coming to Jesus is always the "positive, what-might-be-gained, God-on-a-string" purpose.

What this often means is that, since God's grace abounds, I may now take what is in Scripture and use it to my own advantage. The result is a private theology in which the course of action is determined by what is assessed as being the most beneficial to the person at that moment—by "what makes me feel good."

Such was the Nicolaitan heresy. It is frighteningly timeless, and is alive and well in our own age. Being a personal interpretation it does not take into account the apostolic foundation that personal faith *must be worked out in community.*

How does one spot the tendency to this heresy today? When folk use phrases like "God told me" or "I was led," check the content to see if it has a ring of biblical truth about it. That's a sure tip-off.

What have we discovered about Pergamos so far? Certainly there appears to be some aggressive persecution, for Jesus described the city as the place where Satan resided. The Christian church there presents us with three groups. First, there were Christians who had withstood the temptation of paganism and emperor worship to save themselves harassment. These are described as having kept the faith.

Second, there was an apparently recognizable group who wished to conciliate by showing a "tolerant" attitude toward paganism in the church. These were the Balaamites. Third, there were a number of individuals who claimed Christian liberty as their mandate to be all things to all men. They were, in fact, libertines and though they were probably known to each other, they, in fact, worked individually with

99

an insidious and harmful doctrine they passed on to others. These were the Nicolaitans.

TWO PROMISES

The end of World War II is rather hazy in my mind. I was a child and it seemed that we were always having street parties and private celebrations to announce that the war was over. But my dad had not yet come home from overseas and in the park opposite my home there was still plenty of military activity going on. Time and school history lessons have taught me that what we had, in fact, was a victory in suspension, between D-Day on June 6, 1944, when the war was declared over, and V-E Day, one year later, which was victory day.

Jesus has also proclaimed a D-Day! The war in heaven is won and we celebrate the time leading to the final victory over sin, Satan, and the world. This is a mopping-up operation. Jesus, the passage in Revelation tells us, comes with a two-edged sword against those (Balaamites and Nicolaitans) who do not repent. And He promises a two-edged reward for those who conquer in His name by holding fast the faith.

The first reward is that they will receive some hidden manna (see v. 17), which is understood by many to mean receiving Jesus in all His fullness, hidden from the world but revealed to those who feed on the "bread of life." It is probably another coded promise in which the gift of bread, consecrated as Christ's flesh to nourish and feed hungry souls, is a sign. There is nothing like persistent persecution to make a saint of God hungry for the hidden manna.

The second reward is a promise that occasions much discussion and has produced many theories. It is a promise of a white stone, with a new name written on it, which is an unknown name except to the one who receives it (see v. 17). What is the white stone, and whose name will be on it? Three main theories jostle for acceptance:

1. The white stone represents an entry ticket into a royal banquet. This views the white stone as an entrance to the eternal Eucharist described elsewhere in Revelation as the "marriage supper of the lamb." The name on the stone would then be that of the participating Christian.

2. The white stone represents the acquittal stone used in the law courts. At that period of history a black stone represented a guilty verdict. In contradistinction the stone Christ gives is a sign of acquittal and bears His name as the one who paid the penalty in order that the sinner might go free.

3. The white stone represents purity. This is in keeping with the popular superstition. The white stone, then, represents the purity of Christ given to the believer whereby the recipient receives a new name and a new standing before God.

Each of the three theories retains a certain respectability among scholars. But one thing is certain. The Christians whom Christ commends are those who have not denied His name, but have kept the faith central in their Christian belief and behavior.

A KALEIDOSCOPE OF FAITH

It is self-evident that any attack on the church in Pergamos was exacerbated by its internal dissension. The two sources of that dissension have been a challenge to church life through the centuries. The English reformers William Tyndale and Thomas Cranmer were acutely aware of similar problems in the church of their day, and because it also reflected something of the Pergamos syndrome, it is worth noting their reactions as being perhaps pointers for our own.

The reformers saw plainly that reinstitution of the apostolic office of preaching was essential if their church was ever to deal with heresy. They became tireless and diligent preachers of God's Word. In fact, one might almost say that the Reformation was equally as much about the recovery of preaching as it was an ecclesiastical battle.

Hugh Latimer was, perhaps, the greatest (and wittiest) preacher of the Reformation. His boldness in attacking errors of his day became to antagonists of the Reformation somewhat distasteful. Such preaching usually does become distasteful, and its apostolic truth was probably distasteful to the Balaamites and Nicolaitans in Pergamos also. There, it was only by holding fast the name of Jesus that a true path of faith could be laid against heresy and religious compromise.

The same is true today. Heresy can best be met by teaching Christian truth in the congregation. As pastors carefully, gently, and authoritatively teach believers the way of Christ as revealed in the Scriptures, evangelism, fellowship, good doctrine, and Christian truth will develop a new life in believers, and also guard against heresy.

As in Pergamos, a church will continually be called to repentance for tolerating the nicest of paganism. Christian tolerance in the world church movement brings inherent danger to the church when it has no distinct place for the centrality of Jesus lest His name cause offense to those in whose religion there is no central place for Him.

Pastors, preach the word of God with faith and confidence. Do not compromise, but right where you are preach faith in our Lord Jesus Christ and be with Him an unceasing overcomer in the eternal victory won for us in heaven.

People of God, anybody can live out the mission of Christ and His church when there is no opposition. Coasting downhill with the wind behind you takes no talent whatsoever. But there *is* opposition. Often insidious and often heretical, it calls out in us determination to live out the faith in the church community where life has placed us.

We must start from where we are but we must not pretend that where we are is where we are meant to stay. To try to sanctify the unholy, as some would have us do, is to confuse sophistry with wisdom. We do well to live holy lives so that we shall not be destroyed trying to sanctify what is unholy.

Chapter 6

RESTORING PASTORAL AUTHORITY:
Corrupted Leaders in Thyatira

"And to the angel of the church in Thyatira write, 'These things says the Son of God, who has eyes like a flame of fire, and His feet like fine brass: "I know your works, love, service, faith, and your patience; and as for your works, the last are more than the first. Nevertheless I have a few things against you, because you allow that woman Jezebel, who calls herself a prophetess, to teach and beguile My servants to commit sexual immorality and to eat things sacrificed to idols. And I gave her time to repent of her sexual immorality, and she did not repent. Indeed I will cast her into a sickbed, and those who commit adultery with her into great tribulation, unless they repent of their deeds. And I will kill her children with death. And all the churches shall know that I am He who searches the minds and hearts. And I will give to each one of you according to your works. But to you I say, and to the rest in Thyatira, as many as do not have this doctrine, and who have not known the depths of Satan, as they call them, I will put on you no other burden. But hold fast what you have till I come. And he who overcomes, and keeps My works until the end, to him I will give power over the nations—

'He shall rule them
with a rod of iron;
As the potter's vessels
shall be broken to pieces'—

as I also have received from My Father; and I will give him the morning star. He who has an ear, let him hear what the Spirit says to the churches.""" (Rev. 2:18–29).

MINISTERS OF DESTRUCTION

He was a tall, well-spoken, impeccably dressed young man who came to see the minister about membership in the church. He was also very knowledgeable theologically. But then that was no surprise since he had recently come to the end of a three-year course in theology and prior to that had spent some time in a missionary training college. Nobody questioned that a "prize catch" had arrived to join the congregation, and membership was granted.

The minister was somewhat surprised within the first year of the membership, however, when the young man began to make a number of demands on the church to change its liturgy, its weekly teaching program (of which he himself badly wanted to be the leader), and to limit certain staff ministries. Though he had already been given significant opportunity to teach, he had, in fact, failed to communicate the Scripture effectively and other members had felt compelled to tell him so. He simply rejected that out of hand.

Unknown to anyone in the church eldership, he began to draw a special group around him in an attempt to create something of a private church, which he perceived to be a "deeply spiritual" power group who, he intended, would dominate both church leaders and membership. The effect was to create bitterness and confusion among his little flock, who approached the minister and asked him to act. "You must do something," they pleaded.

The pastor invited one of the church leaders to research the young man's background, something he should have done prior to bringing him into the church. His personal history and Christian pilgrimage, so far as it could be pieced together, was most revealing.

He had held a number of different jobs for only short periods of time. Further, there had already been similar problems with him in other churches, and a demonstrably critical spirit from the college of theology he had recently attended. One faculty member wrote, "He has great potential but somehow always knows, or thinks he knows, just that bit more than his teachers and elders." In short, he felt he had nothing to learn—that he was (in his own self-appointed way) a leader.

When people *independently take authority,* problems multiply. Such was the case in Thyatira.

THE JEZEBEL SYNDROME

It has been said of the Civil War in America that more people died from the results of sickness and disease than died from bullets. More believers died spiritually of the sickness and disease Jezebel brought than from the "bullets" fired by the enemy.

This mysterious creature created enormous havoc in Thyatira. Jezebel was a founding member of the Christianity of feelings.

Emotions are important in worship. Furthermore, even a hurried reading in both Old and New Testaments readily reveals that the people of the Bible were not afraid to worship with their bodies. The psalmist positively encouraged it: "Oh come, let us worship and *bow down;*/Let us kneel before the LORD our Maker" (Ps. 95:6 italics mine). The early Christians were encouraged to pray "lifting up holy hands" (1 Tim. 2:8) and to "greet one another with a holy kiss" (1 Cor. 16:20). In many places in the Bible it is clear that physical dance and body movements, accompanied by happy songs, were recognized as praise and prayer before the Lord.

Our concern here is not so much with the form of worship, though we have much to learn in that direction. Rather, it is with the way a frustrated, strong person who is a non-leader (a person who wants to be a leader in God's church but is yet not called to be so) will take any opportunity available to wrestle leadership away from the appointed leaders, through any possible means. In Thyatira this was done by a Jezebel who appealed to the emotional and physical aspects in worship, stressing improper attention on the body, and easily aroused godless excitement, until it led in the end to worship that was characteristic of paganism. The audacity of this leadership was to describe it as "knowing God in a deeper way" and to use it to undermine the true leadership and gain a personal following.

Saint Paul warned of such leaders in his pastoral instructions to Timothy: "For the time will come when [the people] will not endure sound doctrine, but according to their own desires, because they have itching ears, they will heap up for themselves teachers" (2 Tim. 4:3).

There are *always* religious teachers who are waiting in the wings of the church ready to fit the bill! Not all will be false teachers in the way Jezebel of Thyatira happened to be. They will, however, be people ready to usurp appointed ministerial authority. One of the greatest needs in the twentieth-century church is for the restoration of a true pastoral authority based on a biblical mandate. Such leadership, it seems, was needed in Thyatira also.

A BUFFER TOWN

The well-made tarmac roadway on which our bus had been traveling for hours gave way eventually to the hard-baked mud road of a small village. The town consisted of a few white-painted breeze-block houses, their tin roofs reflecting the glare of the midday sun. Children were playing on the sidewalks. Mothers leaned in the doorways, anxiously watching their offspring but curiously taking note of another busload of religious tourists.

This was Thyatira. Nothing more than a row of peasant houses and one set of traffic lights at the sole intersection.

One could take some comfort in the history books, which record that Thyatira was never an important place anyway. Its sole purpose in being built was to serve as a "buffer town," an early warning system for the great and glorious Pergamos. When the barbarian hordes attacked, it was little Thyatira that was smashed to pieces, "as the potter's vessels shall be broken to pieces" (Rev. 2:27). While the confrontation was still taking place, word was taken from Thyatira along the trade route to Pergamos so they could prepare to repel the attackers.

It is interesting to note, then, that Jesus directed this, His longest letter, to the least important of the towns of the seven churches.

NO IDLE THREAT

We are not surprised, given John's constant use of double meaning in his writings—in Gospel, letters, and Apocalypse—to discover that there is a wealth of hidden inuendo here.

The patron god of Thyatira was Apollo, the sun god, whose eyes were represented as flames of fire and whose feet were depicted as solid burnished bronze. One is not at all surprised that Apollo should be the patron god there, since it was necessary to seek his favors. Pottery, the major trade in Thyatira, required the sun's heat to harden pots for sale in the marketplace. Bad weather meant slow business, so it was essential that the potters keep Apollo *very* happy.

Amazing how economic needs govern the tempo of religious life!

Many Christians, we may deduce from the Scripture reference here, were in the pottery business, and they undoubtedly faced constant pressure to demonstrate solidarity by attending the rites at Apollo's temple. Those rites included pagan sacrifices, demonology, and occultic practice, and while some conceded, not all Christians bent their standards to become involved.

There had been growth there, too. And as in all periods of growth, it became difficult for leaders to keep good control of the membership in matters of Christian doctrine and ministry. It became necessary for a clear word to be spoken to this church and to Jezebel, that gifted leader of people.

Jesus breathed no idle threat, nor was it difficult to understand what he was saying: ". . . the Son of God, who has eyes like a flame of fire, and His feet like fine brass . . . shall rule them with a rod of iron; as the potter's vessels shall be broken in pieces" (Rev. 2:18, 27).

Anyone who had observed the potters' trade firsthand (and that would include most people in Thyatira) knew precisely the extent of the promised punishment. Jezebel's activities would not simply cease, they would be shattered. The judgment came to the church in this buffer town for exactly the same reason as it came to Pergamos, the city for which it existed—namely, for tolerating immorality, paganism, and the occult in its worship and among its members (compare Rev. 2:14 and 2:20).

FACING THE DILEMMA

Is it possible to determine from the biblical text an accurate assessment of what was taking place in Thyatira? One focus was on the question of eating foods sacrificed to idols, an early ethical problem in the church and one about which many Christians were very sensitive.

The problem was this. In the ancient world there were only two places at which meat could be bought. One was the Jewish meat shop and the other the marketplace where meat that had been used in pagan temple worship as a sacrificial offering became available for sale inexpensively.

Imagine the Christian of this period buying meat from the Jewish shop. First, there would be necessary compliance with the religious ceremonies and ordinances of Judaism. Second, there would be the implication that one was part of the Jewish Christendom that required the keeping of certain ceremonial hygiene as a necessary part of one's salvation. Since, in a small town like this one would be known for one's religious affiliation, it would appear most hypocritical to stand in the Christian tradition of "no ceremonial for salvation" and then insist on kosher meat as if it had some intrinsic religious value. It would suggest a partnership with Judaism that Christians were at pains to dispel.

The easiest alternative was to buy meat that implied no such close affinity, and that meant the temple meat. This was still offensive to believers because of the connection with paganism. When Saint Paul had written about the issue earlier (see 1 Cor. 10:14–21) he had appealed to a principle of self-denial for the sake of others, but had inserted a troublesome phrase by suggesting that to eat pagan meat was to partake at the table of demons.

Now, forty years later, the same issue arose, though it did have more sinister overtones than was the case in Paul's day. The questions, however, are the same. The modern counterpart follows the same issue when it poses the statement,

RESTORING PASTORAL AUTHORITY

"It doesn't matter what I do provided I don't hurt anyone else."

The situation with buying meat from the marketplace in Thyatira is not as innocent as it is at first presented. It had clearly reached beyond the stage where meat was the problem, to become one of much greater significance. It seems to have developed into a most beguiling persuasion, which ran something along these lines: "Being a potter, it would obviously help for me to belong to the potters' guild. That means attending the cult festivals. Since the meat I buy from the marketplace does not harm me and since, being a Christian, I do not really believe in Apollo anyway, I can belong to the guild to advantage and blank out of my mind the silly Apollo worship."

ALIBIS FOR EVIL

Experience shows that once the rationalization of sin begins to take place, anything becomes possible. And if that is true for an individual Christian it is equally true for the church. The church today must likewise decide whether to be the spirit of the nation or the body of Christ. It surely cannot be both. If, in being in tune with our culture it thinks to gain acceptance and credibility among the people, it will always decay.

We must certainly start from where people are, but we must not pretend that where they are is where they are meant to be. Christians cannot, however well-intentioned, take on the way of the world, its methods, mindset, or morality, as a way of making God known.

Jesus demands repentance by those so beguiled. Following Jesus always involves complete change in one's way of living, and that comes through repentance. It has been described as a passionate commitment to Jesus Christ.

ENTER JEZEBEL

Thyatira was a growing church. Jesus had much encouragement for the church there, commenting on their good works, Christian love, and continuing faith. How many ministers would welcome such words of commendation from Jesus for their churches and would deserve the encouragement too! What affirmation to the members to hear it said of them that in good works, faith, and service they were actually doing better than ever!

But the guard was down and in walked the spiritual "guru," whom Jesus named "the woman Jezebel," and who described herself as a prophetess. By some manner of means she got herself into a teaching position in the church. We've been here before!

What she was teaching amounted to a syncretistic paganism, which contained enough Christian language to be attractive to some believers. That it is called the teachings of "the deeper things of Satan" is probably sarcasm because she and her followers would surely have called it "the deeper things of God." There are strong indications that it was occultic and certainly contained elements of paganism. Whatever her technique, she had won over the hearts of many people, who Jesus described as her children. Furthermore, her teaching is described as "adulterous" and is said to lead only to sickness and disease. This little profile suggests some basic clues concerning this Jezebel, at least concerning her nature, if not her identity.

On a first reading of the text, Jezebel of Thyatira appears to have been a real woman who exercised influence in the church to an alarming degree. The name could be a pseudonym for a woman who, in the style of paganism, was presenting herself as a Christian priestess. This, inciden-

112

tally, is not such a strange thing when one looks at the situation through the eyes of the religious melting pot of the first century. William Barclay has written about religious prostitution in this way:

> The ancient people were fascinated by what we might call the life force. What makes the corn grow and the grapes and olive ripen? Above all, what begets a child? This is the life force. So they worshipped the life force. But if you worship the life force, then the act of sexual intercourse can become an act of worship; and so temples in the ancient world had hundreds and sometimes thousands of priestesses attached to them who were nothing more than temple prostitutes. [1]

It would not take too much persuading for such a priestess to effect the "worship practice" in Christian circles also, given their recent history in paganism and the accepted necessity of a temple prostitute.

Another view concerning the name Jezebel is that it is a metaphor for a group of Christians practicing a syncretistic religion that tolerated elements of paganism in worship. The metaphor refers to the Jezebel of the Old Testament, the most famous queen of wickedness, who single-handedly led the people of Israel into the cultic worship of idols. This also fits with the mention of adultery in Revelation since the worship of false gods is always called in the Old Testament an "adultery." Reverend Michael Wilcox comments on this aspect:

> The Biblical metapor is that the true God is Israel's husband; the false gods her lovers (Jer. 3, Ezk. 16, Hos. 2, etc.). Jezebel . . . was . . . an outsider who seduced God's bride into this kind of unfaithfulness. [2]

[1] W. Barclay, *Ethics in a Permissive Society* (New York: Harper & Row, 1972) p. 20.
[2] Michael Wilcox, *I Saw Heaven Opened* (London: Inter-Varsity, 1975) p. 49.

The Jezebel of Thyatira also might have been an outsider who was having a catastrophic effect on the church and, again like the Jezebel of the Old Testament, had introduced a mixed theology and practice in religion, which is "adultery" so far as God's people are concerned.

Whatever view you take, "the Jezebel complex" was at work in Thyatira, persuading the church that true religion was the past religious life they knew so well and with which they felt comfortable and secure.

Jesus condemned the church for tolerating this "Jezebel" and warned that the punishment would be exactly the same as that meted out to the ancient Jezebel: the death of her children (see v. 23; 1 Kin. 21; 2 Kin. 9—11).

As Elijah, that monumental prophet of God of Old Testament times, had forced a confrontation with Jezebel over those pagan rituals and had threatened her with death because she had sought to destroy the worship of God, so now Jesus Christ, God's Son, challenged another "Jezebel" in this city of the sun god, where again the worship of the true God was being undermined.

In our time spiritual gurus of the Jezebel variety are still evident, and particularly to be found in the larger churches where they find so much more cover. A shepherd who tends his flock on fifty acres obviously has a better chance to spot a wolf than if he cares for them on five thousand acres.

THE MODUS OPERANDI OF FALSE TEACHERS

A disease is not new simply because we attach a new name to it.

One old pagan disease with a new name is *pluralism*. It is often difficult to recognize because of our readiness to coexist with it in a pluralistic society. Religious pluralism is that paganism which denies the exclusivity of Jesus Christ as the way of truth and life in God.

Another old disease with a new name is *humanism*. This is not secular humanism, which has no place for God, but a religious humanism in which God is cast in the mold of a superman. This divine superman needs our trust and worship in order to exist. In other words, without mankind this god has no value or purpose, for he is our own creation, made in our image.

A third old disease with a new name is religious *occultism*. This consists of a god who is discovered, often by a most tortuous and mystical route, but when found is the recipient of incantation, excess emotional baggage, and is even called upon to judge our enemies. The young man at the opening of this chapter probably fitted most clearly into this brand of paganism. What are the causes of these diseases?

1. *Misuse of Scripture*. God's people cannot be seduced into falsehood if they are strengthened by a living knowledge of God's self-revelation. False teachers only prey on those who know less of the Scripture than they themselves do and are aways beguilers (see v. 26), which is to say that their stock in trade is to mislead people against their better judgment because such people lack knowledge. Well-placed theological persuasion and much used "buzz" words draw a group around such a "knowledgeable" leader, who can then proceed to teach a private brand of paganism depending on what best feeds his ego.

2. *Self-imposed Authority*. Another way to recognize false leadership is the constant appeal by the leader to his own assumed authority (see v. 20).

For three things the earth is perturbed,
Yes, for four it cannot bear up:

115

For a servant when he reigns,
A fool when he is filled with food,
A hateful woman when she is married,
And a maidservant who succeeds her mistress (Prov. 30:21–23).

How wise is the Wisdom Literature! People who give themselves authority usually are unable to accept authority from others. The humility of Christian leadership is possible only as that leader is appointed by the body of Christ. Any other kind of leadership is always dangerous and so often turns into a false leadership. Is it not frightening that Jezebel of Thyatira did not perceive herself as a false leader, but as one whose intention was to teach "deeper things"?

3. *A Refusal to Repent.* A third way to recognize false teachers is their refusal to repent, even when the error of their teaching has been clearly pointed out to them (see v. 21). This is due to their own sense of self-importance and their own privatized understanding of God's call. So arrogant are they that they do not even recognize the biblical requirement of a call from the body of Christ, but simply establish that for themselves. Repentance, therefore, is an unthinkable possibility for them.

There are two places from which false leaders come: from within the church, and from without. Those from without offer a folk religion that is easily recognized and early discarded by most believers.

The more difficult to discern are those who come from within the church (see v. 30), perhaps even faithful Christians who have been members for years. Then, they get a novel slant on the gospel. They perceive doctrinal insight that few other Christians have ever seen. As the text says, they gather a group around them who begin to see themselves as the "true church" within a larger church. It takes a strong biblical leadership in the church at this point to avert a Thyatiran disaster.

Of course, this situation need not be created only by a power group or a powerful person in the congregation. It can also be caused by the minister. Whenever preaching departs from a careful exposition of the text of Scripture and becomes a dogmatic and personalized interpretation, then it is open to all kinds of mischief. When this happens, Christians who are unable to assess the validity of the word preached because of an insufficient knowledge of the Word written, are in a very tenuous position. How can they know the truth? They can be led in any direction, even when such preaching takes place in a church that excels in good works, love, faith, and service (see Rev. 2:19).

I was in a church recently, which grew phenomenally over a short period of years. The preacher was not a false teacher, but he could surely sway his congregation. Shortly after he left, his leading elder said to me, "You felt as if you were walking on air after he had finished preaching. Now that he has gone, we realize that we know nothing of God, Christian doctrine, or our purpose in being a church." Wow! That's dangerously near the edge of trouble.

Although Jezebel of Thyatira was not the minister of the church, she was described as a prophetess. The order of prophet was not usually connected with church leadership, though it was highly respected as a strong spiritual voice. Therefore her opinion would be heard and she would have depended on the gullibility of certain people in the congregation to accept the teachings and the "deeper things" being imparted.

It is always difficult for church leaders to deal with strong personalities when they gather a group around themselves. There are some plausible reasons for this. It is a confrontational act and militates against the strange conception that Christian love and gentleness have no place in pastoral confrontation. A strong, self-appointed leader knows this and presumes upon it.

Another reason is the commonly used one of the pastor feeling threatened by a strong, if self-appointed, leader. With such a rightful emphasis on shared ministry, any pastoral discipline is seen as being judgmental or defensive. At best it is seen as responding to a personal sense of threat and at worst as "stifling the Holy Spirit."

A third reason why pastoral discipline is avoided is the odd notion that the church needs whatever leadership it can get. This view understands leadership in the worldly sense of ability and not in the biblical sense of authority— that is, divinely appointed authority exercised through the church in the choosing of its leadership. You see, the worst position a church can get into is that of giving authority to leaders who claim a personal right to lead based on ability and not on divinely revealed authority. The person who wants to be a leader in God's church simply because he or she has the ability to lead others, and therefore demands a personal right to lead God's people can be extremely dangerous—even a liability in God's church.

All of these possibilities do exist, of course. A pastor *may* feel threatened by a stronger leader. That's the pastor's problem and is not necessarily a cause for disciplining the strong personality who is using initiative in ministry. Confrontation that arises from a personal dislike of a strong member's Christian vocabulary or enthusiasm is not necessarily the member's problem either. It is also true that the church *does* need good leadership among its members, because many pastors are clearly poor leaders.

It is when persons in the church appoint themselves as leaders and teach a Christian faith and lifestyle that are clearly not biblical, that pastoral discipline becomes necessary.

The church of God is called to guard against any teaching that contains enough of the truth to be plausible (at least for the gullible), but contains enough private interpretation to be dangerous to the faith. It is called heresy. It is against *that* we are to guard, even if its proponents appear to be spiritual people with intentions of the highest order. This is, in fact, what makes heresy so difficult to combat.

If preaching Christ and His glory is really the intention of errant teachers, they will listen to biblical defense and be thankful for any correction suggested, re-examining both their thinking and their teaching in the light of those corrections. If it is only their own egos they desire to fulfill, then like Jezebel of Thyatira they will continue using the name of Jesus simply as the device to draw people after themselves and will be uninterested in any correction. In that case, we are dealing with a power complex; and that is why I said it can be found not only among strong leaders in the congregation, but also among many ministers.

HOLD FAST

Let us take our leave of the leaders for a moment and go back to the people, the Christian people, at Thyatira. For there were some who had not been beguiled by Jezebel and who did not follow her new experiential teaching, which they recognized to be a thinly-veiled paganism (see v. 24). They refused to make the adjustments that would make an orthodox Christian faith "more palatable," whether to themselves or to others. Jesus said that dealing with this heresy and its leaders was burden enough and that He would lay upon them no further burden (see v. 25). They were called to hold fast to what they had.

In this very strongly worded passage (see vv. 25–26), the Lord of Glory promised to share His power with those who conquered, telling them that they would have power over nations and would rule with a rod of iron to shatter false teaching as if it were fragile pottery (see v. 27).

How then do we Christians "hold fast to what we have"? There are two essential ingredients. One is *victory* and the other *faithfulness* (see v. 25).

The late Dr. Martyn Lloyd-Jones was a respected and much loved minister of Westminster Chapel, London, where for over a quarter of a century he fostered generations of believers who were well taught and well established in the faith. He often bemoaned the church's preoccupation with Christianity as a spiritual hospital, a counseling clinic where one might find treatment for sickness and a prescription for health. The Doctor (as he was affectionately known) was a medical practitioner and never denied this aspect of Christian ministry, but rather was anxious to demonstrate that the Bible concentrates on the Christian life much more in terms of a battlefield, with commands and orders, where victory is achieved by obeying orders and following one's leader in the battle. In this battle, disobedience of commands leads to chaos and defeat. For the Doctor, much of the "counseling clinic" kind of Christianity was simply evidence of flagrant disobedience. This he discovered from the "spiritual surgery" he performed weekly at his church.

The call to follow Christ is not an invitation to a hospital for the permanent treatment of spiritual hypochondria, which moves endlessly from one symptom to another. The call is to a battle where discipline and obedience are essential if victory is to be gained. Neither does the Christian life consist of one victory at the beginning of the battle. It is a series of campaigns, each different in intensity, and each requiring an ongoing faithfulness to Jesus Christ, the battle leader, who leads us through the veritable minefield of life's gray areas to victory over sin in Him alone. He cannot have disobedience and spiritual hypochondria among His people.

In the matter of victory and faithfulness strong pastoral leadership becomes essential. Let me tell you a story to illustrate that victory and faithfulness to Christ. It concerns a Christian who was most willing to be a part of a pastoral ministry to the sick and housebound. He followed Christ as the One who could heal his own traumatic life, but unfortunately he was easily dissuaded, and when people he visited rebuffed his prescription for dealing with their problems or would not make a personal decision for Jesus, he began to lose heart. He could not see any encouragement in visiting people who would not listen to him, as he thought, and asked the pastor if he could do something more creative in the church's life. From his own traumatic past he felt rejected in his visiting because he needed to control others as a way of validating himself. The pastor explained this and refused the request to do something else, but spent time encouraging the man to exercise patient endurance (see Rev. 2:19), or what we today would call *faithfulness*, and to keep on visiting.

Lord Baden-Powell, the founder of the Boy Scout movement, used to describe faithfulness as "keep on, keeping on"! That's what the man did and he became a favorite visitor whose ministry was much blessed. He was grateful for the strong pastoral leadership that had encouraged him to be faithful to this ministry.

Here, then, are two ingredients necessary to holding fast the faith: one is victory over sin and the other is faithfulness to Jesus and the ministry to which He calls. There can be no place here for disobedience and spiritual hypochondria. The world is a hostile place—a place where the prince of the air, the god of this unbelieving world, works to blind the eyes of those who want to believe in Jesus Christ. The ways of the world are deadly, its people prisoners to sin, and many of its structures deceptive and destructive.

The church at Thyatira experienced success, I'm sure. But it is not success to which the church is called. Many were tolerant to other religious activities. But it is not this tolerance to which the church is called. The church at Thyatira, enjoying its success, appears to have been a very acceptable group. But it is not acceptance to which the church is called. It is to victory in warfare and to faithfulness to Jesus that she is called.

It is to the faithful victors, the conquerors, that Jesus promises to give the "morning star" (v. 28). "As the morning star follows the darkest night," writes Hendrikson, "so the Christians here can look forward optimistically to a dawn of new beginnings." The promise of the morning star is a call to Christians to keep watch over themselves so that through victory and faithfulness they might be ready for the coming of Jesus, that they might also have a part in Him who elsewhere is described as the bright and morning star (see Rev. 22:16).

What greater joy is there for the believer than to know that "when Christ who is our life appears, then you also will appear with Him in glory" (Col. 3:4)? The Christian's aim is to know Christ and the power of His Resurrection. Christ's assurance to the victorious and faithful believers at Thyatira was that they would have that pleasure.

WHATEVER HAPPENED TO THYATIRA?

Jezebel of Thyatira is long dead. But she has many successors. Often they appear as superspiritual leaders of a small power group in the church. Sometimes they appear as mild-mannered but firm spiritual gurus, presenting a manmade theology (not necessarily their own) spiced with exotic experiences and a few "acceptable" biblical texts to justify it. But after that, you create your own pilgrimage!

The rise and fall of ancient Israel reveals a similar pattern. When there was renewal of religious life, it so often was limited to personal gratification of feelings. It had no lasting effect because those feelings were demanding in their insatiability and drove the people of God ever on into more bizarre experiments. History shows that any spiritual awakening that does not pay due attention to corporate worship and knowing God through His Word will always be suspect, and will fall foul to heresy.

The price of carnality and heresy at Thyatira was paid by a congregation who sat open-mouthed, close-eyed, waiting to be fed popular pleasantries in the name of Christianity instead of being about the business of spiritual discipline and ministry for growth in the grace of God.

Jesus says, "He who has an ear, let him hear what the Spirit says to the churches" (v. 11). That means we need to hear when a brother or sister is trying to keep us honest in Jesus. People of God need to hear so they will not lead others into confusion. Pastors in God's church need to hear, for well-placed questions and objections from the people are not always aggression. They could be a way in which God is protecting us against our own heresies, if we have ears to hear. An agitated congregation (and even the self-appointed Christian leadership syndrome) is another way in which God is trying to tell us something. The question is, will people and pastors hear? Do we have enough knowledge of the "combat manual" to know what to do when He speaks in the noise of the battle? Are our eyes so firmly fixed on Him that hearing we shall follow?

Chapter 7

RETURNING TO THE TRUE FOUNDATIONS:
Sudden Death in Sardis

"And to the angel of the church in Sardis write, 'These things says He who has the seven Spirits of God and the seven stars: "I know your works, that you have a name that you are alive, but you are dead. Be watchful, and strengthen the things which remain, that are ready to die, for I have not found your works perfect before God. Remember therefore how you have received and heard; hold fast and repent. Therefore if you will not watch, I will come upon you as a thief, and you will not know what hour I will come upon you. You have a few names even in Sardis who have not defiled their garments; and they shall walk with Me in white, for they are worthy. He who overcomes shall be clothed in white garments, and I will not blot out his name from the Book of Life; but I will confess his name before My Father and before His angels. He who has an ear, let him hear what the Spirit says to the churches"'" (Rev. 3:1–6).

It was Christmas in England, 1981. I was there to visit my very sick father who was undergoing surgery. And it gave me two long weeks in which to spend a happy and memorable Christmas and New Year at home with my mother, who was herself unwell.

The holidays of 1981 were very different from many of the great and hilarious times we had previously experienced. They were instead very quiet and very special. This was the first time I could remember my father's not being there. And, therefore, it was the first time I could recall that he had not followed the ancient English tradition of leaving the house a few minutes before midnight, however cold or wet, and then on the stroke of twelve ringing the doorbell to be welcomed in and to bring with him the New Year. He would be greeted in the hallway first with a kiss from my mother, then hugs and kisses from his seven sons and three daughters, and their wives and husbands.

So this year at the stroke of midnight, which greeted the New Year of 1982, I took over my father's symbolic role. I let myself in to the house in that age-old tradition to wish my mother, who herself was really more ill than we recognized, God's blessing on a year which had begun so painfully. I kissed her, assuring her God was in control, totally innocent of the electrifying impact of what that was going to mean to me and to our whole family.

Towards the end of February, at one o'clock one morning, the telephone rang in our home near Pittsburgh, Pennsylvania. I knew instantly its purpose, for downstairs where I had been working the room had suddenly chilled as if a wind had gently blown through it and left. My brother spoke on a clear line from England.

Mother was dead.

She had seemed to respond to the emergency treatment she received in the hospital over the past three days, and her spirits were high. But suddenly and without warning, her tired heart gave out under the weight of keeping blood pumping to worn lungs. The years of toil and energy in bringing twelve children into the world and raising the ten that lived to mature adulthood had finally closed in. And that faithful Christian spirit was already with the Lord. I was so numbed, I only heard myself saying, "I'm so sorry" and a voice replying, "It happened very quickly—she was gone in a moment."

THE DIVIDING LINE

The line that separates life and death is extremely thin. It is crossed in the twinkling of an eye and often painlessly. I wonder at what point the church at Sardis, which had a name for being alive, passed from real life into death. For Jesus said of this church, ". . . I know your works, that you have a name that you are alive, but you are dead" (Rev. 3:1).

Interesting, isn't it, that an active church is not necessarily alive! The seemingly struggling church with a deadly reputation could be more alive than is often credited, and the church with a lively reputation more dead than we realize. The translation in the *Good News Bible* of the text of Revelation 3:1 is quite pointed: "I know that you have the *reputation* of being alive, *even though you are dead!*"[1]

At what point does a church, or a person for that matter, cross over in that often painless journey from life to death? When do we recognize the moment when one passes from the reputation of being alive, to being dead?

I must confess a professional interest in the questions, having served as a minister in three very different kinds of churches, each with its own special ministries and distinctive lifestyle. I have also worked in ministerial teams who have been very different in their sense of liveliness and Christian life. How does death creep up on Christian experience, and at what points might it be recognized?

For instance, a young man enters the ministry full of vitality, presumably bearing a compelling belief that he is called of God for this service. He works with young people,

---

[1]Quoted from the *Good News Bible*—Old Testament: Copyright © American Bible Society 1976: New Testament: Copyright © American Bible Society 1966, 1971, 1976.

introducing them to the church family and calling them to a personal decision of faith in Jesus Christ.

But after a couple of years ministerial sophistication sets in. The young man, having learned to tumble with the failures and stand high in the successes, attempts another way to interpret the faith in the changing morality in society, because he has become disenchanted with calling people to decision and bringing young people into the church. Society has changed, so he observes, and ministry must begin where people are. Well, that is a primary truth, so the young man takes his theology into Main Street to "bring Christian presence" and not abuse a person's liberty by talking about Christ. Somehow this gospel is to be a contagious disease, which youngsters will catch by being alongside the "Christian presence."

The young minister never seems to notice that it is leading nowhere, and his vocal disillusionment with the church is not recognized by him as a dying gasp as he fights for a Christianity without cost or decision.

He gives up on the church and transfers to community work so that he might "bring Christian presence," and incidentally be paid more money, but that work shows no sign of ever coming to life in the Spirit and making one mark for the gospel in the youth community. He retains all the language and evidence of lively Christianity even as he pronounces the church dead. But who is it that is really dead, and at what point did the fatality begin?

If that is a fair question to ask of an individual, it is an equally fair question to ask of a Christian community also. You see, it is possible to create an image which shouts its own liveliness, thus creating the myth of its reputation, and to maintain such a well-organized machine that few notice that the reputation is merely a shroud over a dead body.

This does not mean of course that every lively, well-managed church is, in fact, dead, but as we look at the church in Sardis we shall notice the signs of a dead church that has only a reputation of being alive.

INOFFENSIVE RELIGION

Sardis, capital of the ancient region called Lydia, lies sixty-five kilometers (about fifty miles) east of the coastal city of Izmir (Smyrna), on what was the busy trade route to the north. Today, the Ankara-Izmir highway runs by the presently named village of Sart. Ancient Sardis was built high on a hill in this mountainous region, but the ravages of time, heavy rains, soil erosion, and earthquakes have left behind only strangely shaped hills and deep valleys. There is little left of the ancient acropolis, though two sites do remain in the valley, one being the temple of Artemis (Diana of the Ephesians), and the other a splendidly renovated Roman gymnasium.

The temple was first constructed in the third century before Christ and twice expanded during the Roman period. The emperor Antonius Pius added a gate to this temple and pronounced that he and his wife be worshiped there as symbolizing Zeus and Artemis. A Byzantine church was built adjoining the temple at a later time, but reflects an earlier period when the church appeared to be in no danger from oppression and could mingle freely, almost publicly, with pagan institutions.

If there is one noticeable difference between the letters to the seven churches, it is that Jesus found something to commend in all but Sardis. In Sardis, apart from the few who were recognized as "not having soiled their garments," Jesus really had nothing to say except, "You have the reputation of being alive, but you are dead."

As simple as that! A word of dread finality! We are not told what gave rise to the reputation, and in the absence of commendation we may not surmise. There is simply a pronouncement of death. Something is desperately wrong. Again, we are not told what it is, though some "divine shorthand," avoiding mention of the civil authorities, can be discerned in the mention of "soiled garments" and "white garments." It is a clue we shall develop in our search for reasons and answers to the reputation enjoyed by the dead church here.

One of the reasons for persecution in the first century was the general tendency to regard Christians as antisocial. They kept their distance from the paganism they had renounced and avoided the social activities and emperor worship that involved idolatry. This was misinterpreted as hatred for the human race. There is, however, no sign of persecution at Sardis, and apparently Christianity was not considered hateful of the human race, but very much a part of it.

One of the supports for that is the small Christian worship house by the temple of Artemis. The present church building was not erected until the late third century, but evidence in many settlements in the province of Asia Minor, in Jerusalem, and in Rome suggests that the early church buildings were erected on holy sites, or sites where Christians had met for secret worship. History provides evidence that the building to be seen presently in the shadows of the great temple at Sardis was erected on the site of a house that Christians had used for worship in the first century.

One is forced to ask how it could be that a Christian worship place would establish itself so close to a pagan temple since Christians, in most places where Rome ruled, preferred a much less public existence. There is no apparent reason for a Christian underground movement here, but it is surprising that they could so openly worship next door to the temple of Artemis.

There is yet another surprise in store. At the far end of the town stood the gymnasium, which has been expertly and lovingly restored by American archeologists under the leadership of Professor M. A. Hanfmann. It covers an area of 22,500 meters square (about 73,125 feet) and reveals a complex of buildings that are symmetrical in design. About A.D. 400 a white marble synagogue was erected within the gymnasium.

The gymnasium itself was a magnificent red stone building whose purpose was more than that of promoting athletic exercise. It was essentially a place of learning and breeding, an exclusive club with a mixture of education, athletics, and religious ritual, intended to create character and a sense of civic duty and pride in succeeding generations. It was also, as you might expect, a place for political gossip and not a little power play. The gymnasium served as an "old boys club" as well as a place of education and the pursuit of character.

The synagogue was not built until the fourth century, and there is no architectural evidence of an earlier one, but its presence suggests that the Jews also enjoyed good relations with their Roman overlords. F. F. Bruce has written the following:

> The imperial ideology was inclusive and tolerant; provided that it received a modicum of recognition it allowed its votaries to please themselves to a great extent in the matter of other religious commitments. But on this point Christianity was exclusive; Christians worshipped God through Christ, and could not pay, or appear to pay, divine honors to anyone or anything else. Their total commitment to Jesus Christ

imposed on them the obligation to be loyal subjects of the emperor and to pray for his welfare, but it forbade them to pray *to* him. (The Jews, in accordance with the first commandment, were similarly debarred by their religion from emperor-worship, but they had long enjoyed specific concessions in this matter from successive emperors.)[2]

How could it be that the Christians, an offensive group to both Jerusalem and Rome, should have such a lively reputation among their neighbors? Could it be that in this particular town, far away from home, and all of them strangers in a foreign land, the citizens of Sardis had come to some measure of religious tolerance that essentially denied the gospel a voice? Indeed, Sardis seems to have been a very pleasant place to live. It could have been an ideal setting for making known the claims of the gospel. But it was much less offensive and disturbing to preach what Nicholas van Hoffman has called the universalistic "mush God," who loves everybody and gives much excitement to His followers. Such a god can be believed without any effect on a life and with no need to proclaim him as the Lord.

In Christian ministry today, this is seen in a contentless gospel, a gospel in which divine demands have been replaced by human needs. It is a gospel tailored to meet "felt needs," beginning and ending with the human dilemma.

Dietrich Bonhoeffer, a martyr of the twentieth century who resolutely refused to accept the contentless gospel, spoke lucidly on the subject:

The world goes on in its same old way, and we are still sinners "even in the best of life" as Luther says. Well then, let the Christian love like the rest of the world, let him model

[2]F. F. Bruce, *Apostolic Defense of the Gospel* (London: Inter-Varsity, 1970) p. 55.

himself on the world's standards in every sphere of life, and not presumptuously aspire to live a different life under grace from his old life under sin. . . . He is doing it for the sake of the world rather than the sake of grace.[3]

It was here that Bonhoeffer wrote his famous paragraph about cheap grace. Because it fits the situation in Sardis and today so well, it bears repeating:

> Cheap grace is the grace we bestow upon ourselves. . . .
> Cheap grace is the preaching of forgiveness without requiring repentance, baptism without church discipline, communion without confession, absolution without personal confession. Cheap grace is grace without discipleship, grace without the cross, grace without Jesus Christ, living and incarnate.[4]

The price to be paid in maintaining a peaceful church with a lively reputation is often a gospel without content. However evangelical its zeal, it is the peace of a graveyard.

WHITE AND SOILED GARMENTS

If the Christians in Sardis had a reputation for being alive, why does Jesus describe them as dead? What caused their demise?

Part of the answer lies with the gymnasium. The reference to white and soiled garments provides us with the clue, so we shall digress for a time and examine the gymnasium. Christians were either members of it or desirous to be, and Jesus referred to it by singling out those who had not been "defiled":

[3]Bonhoeffer, *The Cost of Discipleship*, p. 46.
[4]Ibid., p. 47.

"You have a few names even in Sardis who have not defiled their garments; and they shall walk with Me in white, for they are worthy. He who overcomes shall be clothed in white garments, and I will not blot out his name from the Book of Life; but I will confess his name before My Father and before His angels" (Rev. 3:4–5).

As has been mentioned, the gymnasium was the main place of pagan education, but it was more than that. It was also a forum for adults and a prestigious place for relaxation, philosophical debate, and, no doubt, good business talk. Certainly there was some ritual, especially connected with the athletic endeavor, but it was presumably considered harmless by those Christians who were intent on belonging to the gymnasium.

One entered the gymnasium into a massive foyer, the *palestra,* where a statue of the current emperor, seated, looked sternly down from his niche, and round the walls were inscriptions to famous events, people, and other emperors. Honor was given for athletic prowess and educational or political attainments.

Around the foyer were classrooms, the place for physical education, the library, debating hall, and temple for ritual. Between the foyer and the libraries were the hot baths *(caldarium)* and the cold bath *(frigidarium).* Members would pursue their chosen occupation in the gymnasium, and at some point make their way to the baths, calling in at the changing rooms where soiled garments are divested before entering the hot baths. Conversation took place there, and, as everywhere in the gymnasium, no special claims would be made for any one particular religious viewpoint. From the hot baths members moved to an oval cold-water pool, set in a lovely covered garden where the gossip continued and friendships were reaffirmed. When the cold bath was completed a member was clothed in a fresh white garment, a comfortable, loose-fitting cover in which to stroll the gardens and forge new friendships. In this atmosphere one did not rock the boat with trifling matters like rejecting the ritual or speaking out for Jesus Christ.

It was to these garments Jesus alluded in His careful reference to "soiled and white garments." The gymnasium dominated the town. Everyone belonged to it, whatever their religious convictions. In that temple, dedicated to the worship of man, to speak about Jesus as the Savior of mankind was blasphemy.

What was so wrong with the Christians' belonging to the gymnasium and taking advantage of the educational and social opportunities afforded? Simply, belonging to the gymnasium became an enjoyment in sophisticated paganism. They had laid claim to Jesus Christ and renounced paganism, yet here they were, pretending to be unaffected by the religion of the gymnasium, but clearly being more affected by it than they were able to impress *its* members with the gospel. Somewhere along the line the lively church was dead and the gospel was rendered ineffective. The gymnasium was clearly the enemy about which Jesus spoke. It could be that a form of ascetic Gnosticism had entered the church and a pseudo-Christianity, as F. F. Bruce called it, had ensued.

About Gnosticism, Bruce reminds us that "disparagement of the material order manifested itself in severity to the human body; bodily asceticism and spiritual enrichment." In the Lycus valley of Asia Minor, it seems,

There was a strong inclination on the part of the church to accept an attractive line of teaching which (although they did not suspect it) was calculated to subvert the pure gospel which they had believed and bring them into spiritual bondage.[5]

Do you see what was happening? This intellectual apology for the gospel fitted beautifully into the refined sophistication of the gymnasium. It formed a perfect meeting ground for Christianity, Judaism, and paganism. Christians, looking at the end result rather than the means, did not mind "spoiling their garments" to give the church a lively reputation.

Selling out to the world is still possible. A church that claims faith in Jesus Christ but, in fact, depends on a methodology indistinguishable from the world it says it serves, has in fact become silenced by the system.

Isn't it interesting to note how far the Christian church has moved from its revolutionary beginnings? Instead of believers' studying the apostles' teachings, praying for each other, and proclaiming the gospel in all situations, we now have technique. Listen to this:

> Morale builds through contagious expectancy, good experiences and God-given achievement. A climate of high morale creates optimum conditions for church growth, and church growth in its basic form, is fulfillment of our Lord's central purpose and desire for His church.[6]

I don't know what "contagious expectancy, good experiences and God-given achievement" means, but I'm sure the Christians at Sardis would love the quotation, and indeed so would any copywriter looking for good advertising

---

[5]Bruce, *Apostolic Defense of the Gospel*, p. 66.
[6]W. Arn (ed.), *The Pastor's Church Growth Handbook* (Pasadena: Church Growth, 1981) p. 91.

material for the lively church. Not that many Christians in the first century, except perhaps Sardis, enjoyed "a climate of high morale," but then, Sardis *did* enjoy "optimum conditions for church growth." It was a church with a lively reputation and no doubt part of that was due to the high morale they experienced because their gospel was so much part of the culture.

Christians at Sardis saw no possible harm in accepting the "better" values of paganism, and they were rendered lifeless. Liveliness they might have. Life, they did not.

It is still possible to be silenced by the concessions we make to the culture in which we find ourselves. This is true from the gutter to the country club, from the poorest to the richest, from the least sophisticated to the most sophisticated, from the illiterate to the genius. The Christian is to be independent of the culture, and the church must be especially on guard against opportunism that stems from an attempt to compete with cultural values.

COME ALIVE

But Sardis had a reputation for being alive, so we must continue to press our question, "What gives a dead church a live reputation?" It seems to me that there are two things; one is good publicity and the other is activism. Sardis worked at both. Where members keep telling themselves that they are special people ("movers," who belong to a special place), that will soon spread, and members will go to any length to persuade others to join. The church will grow fat without necessarily growing fit. The people are their own best publicists.

Second, to maintain the image of being alive much activity is required, though little of it need have any spiritual foundation whatever. Busyness fans the reputation for "the movers," who delight in meetings but do very little real meeting. The church with a reputation for liveliness gains it by good publicity (often giving an unreal picture) and by many programs. It also helps to have a good location and no doubt Sardis could offer that also. It was a beautiful place; there were great opportunities for "good" education at a prestigious private school, it was a place of the arts, a place where people were articulate and of important birth or at least important connections. Just the place to be! And it was so lively that its reputation spread far. But it seems little of spiritual significance was taught there for Jesus pronounced the church dead. The preaching must have been acceptable because people came but apparently little was demanded of them, for their lifestyle melted into the culture pretty easily. A church is dead when its "lively" image must be maintained above all else even when "life" is recognizably absent. It is dead when liveliness is more important than truth and when reputation is central to a church's concern rather than the biblical gospel. All of these can be, and often are, stage managed and maintained either by technique or image presentation.

AWAKE, SLEEPER

"Be watchful, and strengthen the things which remain, that are ready to die, for I have not found your works perfect before God" (Rev. 3:2).

Awake! Strengthen! Be perfected! Jesus used words from the gymnasium to apply His message as He challenged His people in Sardis to put as much dedication into learning about Him as they did learning what the gymnasium taught. He urged them to be on the alert for Him because He would come as a thief in the night. He commanded them to look beyond their reputation and face reality about themselves.

So we ask the question again. At what point does a church with a lively reputation cross the line into death? At what point does a church become so man-centered that it is of no earthly use to God? I want to pose three possibilities:

1. *A church is in danger of death when it lapses into self-preservation.* When belonging to a lively church has become a badge of honor, a sign of having arrived, then beware the angel of death. Reputation for liveliness can produce in clergy and congregation alike arrogance and confidence based on their own ability and strategizing. The signs are that the clergy are totally centered on themselves and their church, while the congregation cannot go any further in defending the gospel than to quote what the clergy say.

The rector of a very lively church in England, explaining his success to a group of seminarians, said, "All that is needed to run a successful and lively church is the right place, the right timing, the right speakers. Plan those and the rest will go for you." The right place, of course, was his church, which was in a good neighborhood and a delightful location. The right time referred to both season of year and time of day. Those had to suit the professional, articulate, well-connected members of his church. The right speakers were those few gifted personalities who would draw a crowd—especially from other churches.

2. *A church is in danger of death when it does not recognize its weaknesses.* Historically the city of Sardis had rested secure and arrogant in the supposed belief that no one could destroy or conquer it. The city, after all, was built

138

on a high rocky hill on a narrow neck of land, inaccessible except when approached on the proper road.

There was but one small crevice in the hill guarded all day long, but two hundred years before Christ, intruders had come by night and dealt a crushing blow to the city. It was never guarded at night!

"Awake, and strengthen what remains," said Jesus as He warned the church not to be caught and destroyed at its point of weakness. There can be no sleep when Jesus is Lord. The church is in danger of death when "the Lord" is merely a historic title and not, in reality, Head of the church. When He is not the central Person in the church, *there* may be found the weakest point. When organization, activity, busyness, reputation, and image are central, they are like intruders poised to deal a crushing blow.

3. *A church is in danger of death when it is more concerned with human needs than the worship of a holy God.* It is a wearying operation to keep a lively reputation in a spiritual graveyard, to be sure, for it takes a bundle of recruitment methodology, management technique, and a good public relations system! It increases its passenger lists by offering the church as a clinic in which to get needs met. "Passenger lists" give measurable indications of success, but they also reveal weakness in the church.

More often than we Christians are prepared to admit, the church is in fact called to carry pain in order to discover and worship Jesus Christ as the source of ministry to the world. It is not surprising to find that in Revelation 4 John moved from a focus on the church and its problems to a focus on the Father in heaven.

When Caesar encroaches on a sphere that is not his, as in fact he has been doing in so many places in our own day, Christians, who should be foremost in rendering to Caesar

139

what he might rightly claim, must be foremost in refusing his wrongful claims. For Christians recognize that Jesus Christ their Lord is "the ruler of kings of the earth". . . .[7]

But Caesar has been allowed to invade the church. Without raising a finger he has dislodged Christ as the head of the church (see Eph. 4) and replaced Him with human dilemmas. Caesar can manage and maintain the church well this way, but at the expense of being dead to the voice of Christ.

We need to be afraid when people speak well of us for it is a sign we may simply be meeting their human needs. God's church is called into being to worship Him in spite of hurts and needs.

FINDING LIFE AGAIN

Writes Maurice Nesbitt about psychological fear, "There is warfare here; and what we are after is not an easy truce but a decisive victory."[8] Such was also true in the church at Sardis. Jesus moved among the churches (see 2:1), apparently searching for something better than an easy truce with Caesar. He was looking for faithfulness to the Father among those who claimed to be His followers. It was because He had not found faithfulness at Sardis, but only a reputation for liveliness, that he summarily declared the church dead. To this point He complained sorrowfully, "I have not found [discovered] your works perfect before God" (3:2). The word "discovered" here is the Greek word *eureka*, which suggests a picture of one expecting to uncover a great find. Sardis might be a great discovery for those who

[7]Bruce, *Apostolic Defense of the Gospel*, p. 59.
[8]Maurice Nesbitt, *Where No Fear Was* (New York: Seabury, 1979) p. 59.

were looking for liveliness. When Jesus looked for life and faithfulness, He discovered only death.

He offered a way to rectify the situation. That way was repentance. Jesus called them back to first base, to what they had already heard and believed (see v. 3). They could not bring their reputation, liveliness, or even great size (if it was indeed a large body of believers), but they could only come in repentance.

Believers can never afford to get away from the shadow of the cross, just as unbelievers can come to God no other way than through the cross of the Lord Jesus Christ. We never grow so strong, so powerful, so mighty, or even so lively that we can leave the cross behind.

Repentance means to "let go" or "turn around" on the understanding that the past way has been wrong and must be dropped totally and forever. God does not deal in moral terms of good and bad here, but in legal terms of right and wrong. It is possible to be good but very wrong! Sardis was a "good" church if reputation for liveliness was anything to go by. It was a desperately wrong church, for whatever it preached or however it lived, Sardis was certainly not right before God. And in not being right it had died.

Sardis was called back to square one. "Let go of everything in which you have trusted for your reputation and life, and exercise grief for having gone that way, Sardis," Jesus seems to say, "for like the night attackers of your history, 'I will come upon you as a thief, and you will not know what hour I will come upon you'" (3:3).

The gospel is bad news before it is good news; it is death to sin before it is a life of faith. "In the parable of the prodigal son," writes Nesbitt, "it isn't so much that someone gets lost, like a man in a fog or snowstorm, but that the youngest brother deliberately walks out of his father's house, and it

141

takes him a long time before he realizes the nature of his predicament."[9]

Sardis was not the first church that had to pay dearly for remembering a religious text that was convenient to its inclination while forgetting a biblical idea it found too exacting. "Turn to me," said Jesus. "Repent and believe" (see Mark 1:14–15). So again He said to Sardis, "Remember therefore how you have received and heard" (v. 3), and what they had received and heard was that repentance leads to life. They can hardly have been surprised to hear Jesus say again, "Hold fast and repent" (v. 3).

AN OLD-FASHIONED WORD

What does it mean to repent? Let me explain it this way. A piece of coal falls from the fire into the hearth, a blackened, smouldering mass. The daring young man lifts the coal quickly with two fingers to flip it back into the fire. But the coal has not lost its heat and the young man, his fingers painfully tingling, makes two split-second decisions: one, he should never have picked it up in the first place; two, he won't do that again!

That is repentance. It is a declaration of intent, made in the light of an action or actions in the past, that will affect not only the present but, intentionally, the rest of one's life.

Popularity, success, and liveliness are not signs that all is well with God. Faith, rest, and confidence in Jesus are the signs to look for. And these come as we depend upon and worship the Father, for it is there that we are provided with the only place of certainty.

[9]Ibid., p. 20.

THERE'S SOMETHING LEFT

One can almost hear the sigh of relief in Jesus' words: "You have a few names even in Sardis . . ." (3:4). There were still some, only a few it is true, who had not been carried away with the lively reputation of the church to which they belonged. There were still some who had not sought the acclaim of the white garments of the gymnasium as the price to be paid for that lively reputation.

They were still discovering faith and life in their worship of Jesus as the source and sustainer of life. The first work of the church is worship. We are called into being as a worshiping community who have come to Jesus to be "built up a spiritual house" (1 Pet. 2:5). Archbishop William Temple wrote concerning worship,

> Worship is the submission of all of our nature to God. It is the quickening of conscience by his holiness; the nourishment of mind with His truth; the purifying of imagination by his beauty; the opening of the heart to his love; the surrender of will to His purpose—and all this gathered up in adoration, the most selfless emotion of which our nature is capable and therefore the chief remedy for that self-centeredness which is our original sin and the source of all actual sin.[10]

The cause of decay at Sardis was not opposition or paganism, but a "self-centeredness which is our original sin and the source of all actual sin."

But there were some who had not soiled their garments, who in worship had submitted all of their lives to God.

[10]William Temple, *Readings in Saint John* (London: Macmillan, 1939) p. 68.

These would "walk with Me in white, for they are worthy" (3:4), said Jesus. May we, in our day, repent of our religious gymnastics and return again to the heavenly altar of God and praise Him for His mighty works!

Chapter 8

REWARDS FOR THE SAINTS:
Perseverance in Philadelphia

"And to the angel of the church in Philadelphia write,
'These things says He who is holy, He who is true, "He who
has the key of David, He who opens and no one shuts, and
shuts and no one opens": "I know your works. See, I have
set before you an open door, and no one can shut it; for you
have little strength, have kept My word, and have not denied My name. Indeed I will make those of the synagogue of
Satan, who say they are Jews and are not, but lie—indeed I
will make them come and worship before your feet, and to
know that I have loved you. Because you have kept My command to persevere, I also will keep you from the hour of trial
which shall come upon the whole world, to test those who
dwell on the earth. Behold, I come quickly! Hold fast what
you have, that no one may take your crown. He who overcomes, I will make him a pillar in the temple of My God,
and he shall go out no more. And I will write on him the
name of My God and the name of the city of My God, the
New Jerusalem, which comes down out of heaven from My
God. And I will write on him My new name. He who has an
ear, let him hear what the Spirit says to the churches"'"
(Rev. 3:7–13).

The bus was cruising along a new, swift highway which,
judging by its emptiness, was rarely used. A minor earth
tremor had occurred the previous day, and our eyes were
riveted to a scene a few hundred yards away which we
thought might be connected to it. Three columns of smoke

145

were curling their way upward into a bright blue sky. Had the earth cracked? Was it the aftermath of some disaster?

As the road curved gently, we were drawn nearer to the answer to our questions. Smoke was rising from wells of boiling water. There were many such smoke pillars in the area, but these were the three largest; and though they looked only a few yards away, they were in fact a few miles away across the flat fertile plain.

WELCOME TO PHILADELPHIA

We were near Philadelphia. That reminded me . . . the biblical text concerning Philadelphia talks about being a pillar, and not going "out" anymore. "He who overcomes, I will make him a pillar in the temple of My God, and he shall go out no more" (3:12).

I had always thought that was a strange phrase. How could an immovable pillar go out? But when I saw the hot springs, it all began to piece together.

You may remember we said earlier that Saint John hallmarked his knowledge of the churches to which he was writing by attending to some specific features of each city. That feature in Philadelphia was connected with the geophysical nature of the area in which it was built.

Minor earth tremors in Turkey are quite common, and the hot water springs are a reminder of this geophysical activity. In John's day, the city of Philadelphia suffered much from the tremors, and the residents lived in constant readiness to pack their bags and leave because the earthquakes repeatedly damaged the city. The pillars would come crashing down with the buildings as the people rushed here and there to escape the debris. They were, it seemed, forever "going out" from one tremor after another.

The text began to fall into place. To be a secure pillar in

the house of God was an appealing promise to a group of Christians who were ever at the mercy of a fallen earth. Thus, Philadelphia introduces us to a set of Christians who teach us perseverance in the face of powerlessness from both man and nature.

THE TALE OF TWO BROTHERS

One hundred fifty years before Jesus was born, there were two brothers whose excessive loyalty to each other so impressed everyone that they were nicknamed *philadelphoi*, "brother-lovers." Their names were Attalus II and Eumenes. To honor their loyalty to each other, a city was established in the ancient world and dedicated to them. It was called Philadelphia. The name was formed from an amalgamation of two Greek words, *philos* which means "affection," and *adelphos*, meaning "brother."

It is interesting, then, that the matter of loyalty forms the foundation of the message from Jesus Christ to the Philadelphians of the first century: ". . . you have a little strength, have kept My word, and have not denied My name. . . . I also will keep you from the hour of trial" (3:8,10).

The city was originally founded for the express purpose of spreading Greek thought and civilization throughout the province. But the solidarity of the barbarians there made Philadelphia a failure as a cultural endeavor. Sardis, which was built for a similar purpose, had much greater success as we have seen. *They* even managed to establish a Roman gymnasium (the epitome of Greek culture) for the propagation of civilized education and debate. Philadelphia had no such record.

All that now remains to remind the visitor that this had once been an important trading place with a most gracious foundational history is a few hundred feet of the ancient city wall, and that from the late second century. The columns of one arch from a fourth-century church, with a faded fresco of Jesus in the style of Orthodox iconography, tell us that the church succeeded here for some time after the late first century. The motif, then, is a pertinent one for the city, and particularly for the Christians there, who were powerless to do anything. Jesus had a word of comfort for His people with His promise that those who were faithful to His name would defeat oppression and "never go out." It was a promise of security, of a final reward for loyalty.

THE CAUSE OF POWERLESSNESS

If the ravages of nature rendered the Christians, along with everyone else, powerless, there was also another reason why those believers particularly were left without much strength. Saint Paul was hounded by Judaizers on his missionary travels, and it was they who finally set in motion the series of events that eventually led to his house arrest and death. The Judaizers were also behind the problems faced by Christians at Smyrna and at Philadelphia. Just who were these foes?

They were Jews, offended by the new sect called Christianity because of its disregard for Jewish food laws and old covenant ceremonial ritualism. The dangerous element for Christians was that many Judaizers were quasi-believers in Christ who held very sincerely to the view that Christianity should not dispense with the Jewish rituals and observances, but place them instead at the very center of Christian faith.

All those years prior to Saint John's visions for the church, Saint Paul had preached endlessly the doctrine of Grace—God's unmerited favor—as the basis for knowing

Christ and maturing spiritually. "By the deeds of the law no flesh will be justified in His sight" (Rom. 3:20), he had written. And to the Christians at Ephesus he had made the case equally clear: "For by grace you have been saved through faith, and that [faith] not of yourselves; it is the gift of God, not of works [that which we do], lest anyone should boast" (Eph. 2:8–9).

We can offer nothing to God, not even our religious observances, in exchange for salvation. It is a gift from God, through the faith He supplies, in order that we may believe. Neither can we, having exercised that faith toward God, add anything to make it more effective.

So here was a religious legalism, a hybrid mix of Judaism and Christianity, a battle still raging a generation after Paul. There was great confusion and pain. Again in Philadelphia we see a church handicapped by those who claimed to be the most concerned for her welfare. Then as now, major setbacks for the church were created by people who made religious causes an excuse for war, but who themselves were not obedient to the church's true message and ministry. In Philadelphia, the religious war of Saint Paul's day was still going on.

We have no indication that the Judaizers did actually belong to a synagogue or any particular church. They are simply described by the Lord as being false Jews belonging to the "synagogue of Satan."

PARA FAITH

Perhaps the real problem with the false Jews was that they, in fact, belonged nowhere. Perhaps they were free floaters who had developed a theology of their own, following their own leaders and not committed to the church of God in any way. We have similar situations today with churchless Christians and the end result of this spiritual aberration is death. You cannot have the head without the body, for Christ is not divided.

These "Jews who are not Jews" claimed for themselves privileges before God that they felt were already theirs because of their racial descent and religious ritual. It was that issue to which Jesus spoke, describing Himself as the only true and holy One—"He who has the key of David, He who opens and no one shuts, and shuts and no one opens" (Rev. 3:7).

The idea here comes from Isaiah 22:22, where the king is described as God's servant in whose possession is the "key to the house of David" and in whose power it is to open or shut the door. Once open or shut there can be no reversal. Jesus now took this authority on behalf of the believers in Philadelphia, encouraging them with His words: "I have set before you an open door and no one can shut it" (Rev. 3:8). For the Judaizers this was a reversal of order, for they held that God had, after all, promised to King David and his descendants that He would love *them* with an everlasting love exclusively. Now He was saying that it was the Christians He loved: ". . . indeed I will make them [the Judaizers] come and worship before your feet, and to know that I have loved you [Christians]" (Rev. 3:9).

Jesus was affirming believers—Jews or Gentiles—who knew and worshiped Him alone for salvation and who recognized Him as Lord of the church, as those who would possess eternal life. This is the proper vindication that belongs to the Lord alone. "Shall not the Judge of all the earth do right?" asked Abraham (Gen. 18:25). Of course He will, and He will always vindicate the saints who persevere. His promise to set before them an open door (v. 8) is coupled with "I have loved you" (v. 9) to vindicate them, and to give hope and assurance. God is in control. He does nothing by accident. We can therefore persevere both with patience and with faith!

THE POWER OF GOD

So Jesus commended them: "For you have a little strength, have kept My word, and have not denied My name" (3:8). Though they had been rendered powerless in human terms, they had retained the strength to maintain their faith.

The oppressed, or powerless, are a special concern of the church of Christ, and rightly so. Powerlessness leaves a person or a group with no voice against oppressors and no strength to escape them. Jurgen Moltmann wrote, "The identification of Christ with the poor and His brotherhood with the very least, belong, according to Matthew 25, within the framework of a coming judgment."[1]

Powerlessness, often identified with the poor, is a tragedy made worse when it goes unrecognized by those with power to help make changes. Ask the impoverished citizens of a densely populated urban area of any major city. They will tell you of the stranglehold of powerlessness. "What can we do?" they ask. "Decisions are made about us and our area by people who do not even live here. But what bargaining position do we have? No one wants our opinions."

Perhaps this was the feeling of Christians in Philadelphia, too. Cornered, oppressed, and with little strength to stand against the opposition, they could have been forgiven some self-pity as they reviewed their powerlessness.

---

[1]Moltmann, *The Church in the Power of the Spirit*, p. 301.

THE MEANING OF POWER

Power has two meanings. It is a word we use when we speak of someone's having the strength to move a heavy object. For example, we think of a weightlifter or an athlete as being powerful. When used in a New Testament setting, this word is *dunamis*, from which we get our word dynamite. It speaks of God's power as explosive in nature, His divine energy if you will, able to change lives.

The other use of the word power is in terms of authority. This New Testament word is *exousia*. It speaks of authority inherent in a role or office. The president of the United States of America possesses in his office the authority needed, for example, to defend the Constitution. It was this second word Jesus used at Philadelphia when He said, "You have a little strength."

It is only as we recognize that human influence and expertise will not take us through His open door, that Christians ever discover God's authoritative power to fulfill His purposes in the world. The church, it is true, may not appear to be strong in the world. It has often lacked visible authority. But that in no way destroys the truth that God is in control and that Jesus still opens doors for those who keep His word and do not deny His name. It is "a little strength," as the world sees it, but for believers it is the way through a door that Jesus opens and no one can shut!

Ivy Harris was an ordinary person. When I first met her she was learning to cope with a new and difficult handicap; she had gone blind as an adult.

Naturally, this handicap was a great distress to her, causing enormous readjustment in her life. She found herself living in altogether new spiritual and psychological battlegrounds. She had a "little strength," with a faith that did not deny the name of Jesus, but rather kept His Word with determination. Amid the confusion and challenges, Ivy proclaimed continuously the sufficiency of Christ for all her needs. Perhaps blindness, even in middle age, could become God's door of opportunity. Indeed, He who had seen her works was setting before her an open door.

Across town, Dorothy Neale had cared for her blind mother for years. She had become her eyes and ears to the world. When her mother died, it took some time for Dorothy to readjust. She was now left on her own, seemingly of little service to anyone, but with a lot of experience in dealing with the blind. By God's magnificent though often painful route, His door of opportunity opened to draw Dorothy Neale and Ivy Harris together. Dorothy had the gift of helps, Ivy had a need. In His expansively gracious ways God used their "little strength" for ministry in the neighborhood.

We may think we have little strength in the church, but as we keep God's Word and do not deny His name, we will be surprised at the doors He will open—doors which no one can shut. And one day, seeing God's power in our weakness, all people will bow down before the believers' feet recognizing that Jesus has indeed loved His people (see Rev. 3:9).

TWO KINDS OF BELIEF

We have used the phrase from verse 8 quite often in this section: "You . . . have kept My word, and have not denied My name." Let us now examine what it means and what it *can* mean for a Christian, for it becomes a key phrase to victory in the world for the church of God. The word *kept* speaks of faithfulness and perseverance, or "patient endurance."

Perseverance in faith is a terrific idea when all is going well in life. But it is proven best when one is struggling uphill. If we are honest with ourselves we readily recognize that it is easy to convince people about Jesus Christ, but it is incredibly hard work to keep them growing in faith. It's easier to catch fish than it is to clean them! A friend once claimed that he could have a 99 percent success rate in leading people to Christ and a 1 percent success rate in keeping them there. Perseverance in faith almost seems a forgotten art.

There is one kind of Christianity that needs to be constantly fed with razzmatazz experiences. There is another kind that aims to keep people very involved in lots of programs and church activity as a way of holding Christians in the faith. In both cases people are so busy fulfilling themselves that they close their eyes to the reality of any other existence until some crunch point arrives. Then, finding they cannot cope with it, they rush off to find someone else's answer to the problem.

There is a third choice—a biblical Christianity in which believers get to know God's Word, keep it, and remain faithful to Jesus Christ. Often this will be ridiculed or challenged. Sometimes difficult situations will arise. From time to time the going will get very tough from many angles at once. The weariness of standing against the Devil and all his works will tempt the believer to "drop out," or even persuade one that "this Christianity business is too hard!" But perseverance in faith, regardless of "little strength," enables the believer to keep God's Word and not deny His name.

Joining the church in Philadelphia was one thing; persevering with it was quite another! They had, humanly speaking, good reason to abandon ship. But God, who by His own grace had drawn those saints to Himself, is in control of all things, and He opens the door of His city *to those believers who patiently endure to the end*. As then, so now.

What a strange picture of power this is! I have the slight suspicion that Christianity in the West, influenced by its culture, has suffered from a mistaken idea of power based on aggression, size, leadership, and manipulation.

Dr. Win Arn took a look at Campus Crusade's "Here's Life America" program. "Here's Life" was an evangelistic program in which Campus Crusade took their imaginative campaign for the gospel to metropolitan areas and smaller communities. Dr. Arn reviewed the resultant publicity:

> Consider this statement of [Bill] Bright, who calls "Here's Life America" the "greatest spiritual harvest in the history of the church. 100 times—yes, 1,000 times—greater than anything I have ever seen or read about in the almost 2,000-year-old history of the church."
>
> Overkill? I think so. I can hardly believe he has never heard of the early church—or of the rise of the Protestant Reformation—the Wesleyan Movement—or more currently the movement of God in Africa.[2]

Win Arn describes such publicity as a fantasy and a fog. The power of God is seen not in a fanfare of publicity or (dare I say it?) in large, powerful, manipulative religious programs, but in the perseverance of saints in the midst of opposition. The Christians at Philadelphia gained special praise from Jesus for their "insignificant ministry," with a little strength, which became mighty because it was rooted in God's Word and did not deny His name. Countless programs have come and gone while the church, with all her problems, still remains.

[2]Arn, *The Pastor's Church Growth Handbook*, p. 5.

"DOING" THE WORD

Jesus often spoke to His disciples on this theme of might through perseverance. His Sermon on the Mount, for example, is full of such reversals. He calls people to hold dear the very things others have rejected or despised. We have only to think of the Beatitudes, "beautiful attitudes," which were totally opposite to the attitudes normally adopted. Or the more obvious "turn the other cheek" saying. As the Sermon comes to a close (Matt. 7:24–29), He says, "whoever hears these sayings of Mine, and *does them*, I will liken him to a wise man who built his house on the rock" (italics mine).

Hearing the Word of God only brings power when Christians *do* the teachings of Jesus. Keeping the Word means doing what Jesus teaches. For the believers in Philadelphia that meant "turning the other cheek." They had heard Saint John teaching them the words and works of Jesus (the apostolic faith as we call it), and remembered the teaching about being reviled without reviling again and walking the extra mile. Now they found that as they *did* the teaching of Jesus, so they were keeping His Word.

We may take a lesson from them in our twentieth century. Do we Christians find ourselves again challenged to keep God's Word in the morass of a changing society? Is it not so often true that anything that challenges our desires, our way of life, our church fellowship, our possessions or our intentions, is conveniently reinterpreted to fit in with our plans?

Many Christians handle Scripture in just that way and defend their actions with a theology that says, "I can interpret the Bible my way, and you, yours!" With blatant plurality, we defend disobedience to the Word of God by saying that this is the twentieth century and life is different now. Listen to Maurice Nesbitt:

> The words of Jesus, in particular, contain a spiritual potency which goes far beyond their surface meaning. "The words," says Jesus, "that I speak unto you, they are spirit, and they are life." We must drink in His words as we would a glass of wine. We must also eat and digest them as we would our daily food. We must carry them about with us as we would the coins in our pockets. We must memorize them as we would our own address, or the license plate of our car. We cannot expect to have faith in God if we do not have faith in the words which God speaks to us.[3]

Conveniently, Jesus' confrontation with the rich young ruler does not fit in with our commercial economy; His meeting with the adulterous woman is simply a lesson to hypocrites; His dealing with the leprous outsider is a good picture of love because we do not have to deal with lepers.

Doing the teachings of Jesus, you see, can mean an intrusion into a comfortable life by a mass of troublesome humanity tugging at your coat, abusing you, making demands, treating you as a doormat. Michel Quoist catches the essence of "doing the teachings of Jesus" perfectly in one of his meditations:

> As a ray of sun slips in unnoticed Your grace has stirred me—and rashly enough I left my door ajar. Now Lord I am lost! Outside men were lying in wait for me. I did not know they were so near; in this house, in this street, in this office, my neighbor, my colleague, my friend. As soon as I started to open the door I saw them, with outstretched hands, burning eyes, longing hearts, like beggars on church steps.
>
> The first ones came in, Lord. There was after all some

[3]Nesbitt, *Where No Fear Was*, p. 46.

space in my heart. I welcomed them—You would have been pleased Lord, I would have served and honored you in a proper and respectable way. But the next ones, Lord, the other men; they were hidden behind the first ones—they drag the world behind them with everything rusted, twisted, or badly adjusted—I can't stand it anymore! It's too much! It's no kind of life! What about my job? My family? My peace? My liberty? And me? Lord, I have lost everything, I don't belong to myself any longer; there's no more room for me at home.[4]

Doing the teachings of Jesus has been replaced with a starvation diet of entertainment Christianity, which must constantly be updated. We have failed to build the church on the foundation of obedience to God's Word, or even to encourage one another in it. Consequently, human management techniques, exclusive friendship clubs, and harmless sermons—together with lots of personal attention in the style of the counseling clinic—have become our legacy. We will listen to and accept anything if it is presented excitingly enough. Indeed, have you noticed how the word *exciting* has slipped into our church vocabulary? We talk about "an exciting church, "an exciting program," or "an exciting minister," but rarely of "an obedient church."

Christians in Philadelphia were surrounded in their day by a world not so far removed from ours. It was a commercial world, a world of all shades of gray, a bustling, rushing world with its own variety of religious options. They, too, were forced to face issues, make difficult decisions, and live on the edge of dilemma. We are not the first to face those pressures. They, too, were powerless and without influence.

[4]Michel Quoist, *Prayers of Life* (Plainfield, N.J.: Logos, 1963) p. 47.

What would they do? Save their necks by popularizing the gospel? Should they search out opportunities to be influential in the community, or to be a powerful force with authorities? What they did instead was *simply keep God's Word*. They persevered in faith rather than seek power. They remained obedient to what they had learned and practiced the teachings of Jesus among themselves, even though it was contrary to what might be deemed success and influence.

How incredibly basic! Faced with certain ridicule, they were obedient to the Word of God. Jesus commended that kind of spiritual maturity.

The second thing which Jesus singled out for praise, because it is a necessary ingredient of victorious Christian living, is summed up in the phrase "You have not denied My name" (v. 8). Let me illustrate that ingredient in a simple story of an occasion that has proved to be one of the most profound in my own ministry.

Michael and Caroline had been, from the first week of my ordained ministry, great friends and counselors. When their fourth child, Philip, was but one year old, Caroline discovered she had an illness diagnosed as terminal. It could be stayed awhile, however, if she would submit to a painful and nauseous two-year treatment. Michael, together with one of my assistant pastors and I, laid hands on her and prayed for her deliverance. God graciously healed her at that time. She recovered, to live a further seven years before the illness struck again with hardly any warning.

After some weeks of being confined to her bed she began to deteriorate. I visited with her to pray and always found her a brave soul. Those were precious moments. It was clear that she was facing death. It would not be easy for any of us, but she did not deny His name even in her pain and frustrations.

159

On my last visit I read to her from Psalm 73:28: "But it is good for me to draw near to God;/I have put my trust in the Lord GOD,/That I may declare all Your works." Three hours later she was in the presence of the Lord.

The whole family shared her confidence. Sure, there was sadness. There was pain. But I have never seen a family so prepared for death and peaceful throughout the whole experience.

That is the reward of faithfulness.

It was that kind of perseverance—patient endurance—that marked out the Christian community at Philadelphia. They knew the pressures; they lived with what the world calls powerlessness. But they held fast to Jesus with a perseverance that showed a powerful Christian integrity developing in those who kept His Word and did not deny His name. They would be obedient and faithful to what they had heard and received.

A DAY OF VINDICATION

Where did it all lead in the end? It must sometimes have seemed to the Philadelphians that the war would never be over—as indeed it has often appeared to Christians through the ages. Nothing could be further from the truth. The war in heaven is over; victory is assured.

One day God will vindicate His followers by bringing to their knees those who presently oppress them, and He will open a door of opportunity for His saints. But it will also be a door into a secure dwelling place, a new Jerusalem.

Vindication is the knowledge that the God of all the earth will do right. The early Christian leader Tertullian (who subsequently departed from the faith) seemed to mistake it for vengeance when he wrote with great relish at the thought of seeing philosophers roasting in hell before their students; of seeing kings, who were supposed to be appointed by God and who, therefore, ought to know better than most, writhing for freedom from the flames and crying out to those whom they had persecuted.

Vindication is the sure knowledge that God will not fail His children. When it is all over and the dust has settled, however wrong we judge our opponents to have been, we all face God. He will do no wrong. Sometimes, it is true, God's vindication takes place in a lifetime. But until it does, our job is simply to persevere, keeping God's Word and not denying His name.

It is here, in the text, that practical theology meets an incredible prophecy: "Because you have kept my *command* to persevere, I also will keep you from the hour of trial which shall come upon the whole world, to test those who dwell on the earth" (Rev. 3:10 italics mine). We have met this impending doom before (see 2:10) and it suggests a further persecution is forthcoming on the known world of the Roman Empire. They were told, "Hold fast what you have," which suggests that what they had would keep them in that day of trial.

A GLORIOUS REWARD

Here, then, was a company of God's people who were said to already possess a divine crown of glory. They lived in a situation of powerlessness and suffered because of the tongues of Judaizers. They were warned that a great trial was coming which would bypass them, but on the other hand, they had their bags packed permanently in readiness for flight from earthquake or barbarian attack.

Against all this they had refused to degenerate into a grumbling community of believers. The choice was never to demand from God release or to throw away the faith.

Instead, with patient endurance, they had kept God's Word and had not denied His name. Thus the divine promise came. "He who overcomes, I will make him a pillar in the temple of My God, and he shall go out no more" (v. 12).

In a city where people were ever on the move, the promise to be made "a pillar in the temple of My God" came as a promise of incredible security. King David, the great Jewish king, longed for his people to dwell in the house of the Lord their God, all the days of their life, and to see the beauty of the Lord and understand His temple (see Ps. 27:4). In heavily Jewish apocalyptic language, Jesus demonstrated to the faithful that God was with them. He had marked them. He would be with them to strengthen them. They would be pillars in the temple of God, marked with the name and city of God.

No one who has visited the Holy City can miss the implication here of the promise of God's glorious power and presence. Jerusalem has always been known as the City of God. Physically, it is constructed upon solid rock. It is beautifully situated. Even in Philadelphia's day, it was probably the oldest inhabited city in the world.

Spiritually, Jerusalem has always been a symbol to believers of God's dwelling place, whose doors He alone opens and no one shuts. In the Philadelphian letter, God came to His beleaguered people in such beautiful apocalyptic language. He came, in a phrase often used in Revelation, to "write on him My new name."

This is ever the Christian's confidence. The church is not called to make Jesus relevant, to represent Him in high places, to make Him popular, or to gain great power and influence in the world. She is called by His grace to follow Him, to do His Word, to hold fast His name in whatever situation she faces.

Jesus has marked us with "the name of My God," and to

those who persevere He "will write on him My new name."
It is the believers who finish the race who will be with Jesus
in the temple of God, eternally secure.

Writer David Watson, in his book *I Believe in the
Church*, has a chapter devoted to discussing the army of
God. He says, "We are not playing religious games; we are
not even fighting against flesh and blood. We are contend-
ing against an immensely powerful spiritual army and we
need to realize our total weakness without God."[5]

Christians at Philadelphia knew that. They became well
aware that perseverance in the faith was far more powerful
than political or personal influence might have been. They
also knew it had greater significance, for perseverance is
commanded by Jesus, not simply invited as an option.

Do not ever quit. Resist that temptation to bail out which
appeals to all of us at certain times. Stay with Christ. Stay
with His church. No matter what!

[5]David Watson, *I Believe in the Church* (Grand Rapids: Eerdmans, 1979) p. 153.

Chapter 9

GOD'S CONSTANT GIFT OF MERCY
The Doorway to Warmth in Laodicea

"And to the angel of the church of the Laodiceans write, 'These things says the Amen, the Faithful and True Witness, the Beginning of the creation of God: "I know your works, that you are neither cold nor hot. I could wish you were cold or hot. So then, because you are lukewarm, and neither cold nor hot, I will spew you out of My mouth. Because you say, 'I am rich, have become wealthy, and have need of nothing'—and do not know that you are wretched, miserable, poor, blind, and naked—I counsel you to buy from Me gold refined in the fire, that you may be rich; and white garments, that you may be clothed, that the shame of your nakedness may not be revealed; and anoint your eyes with eye salve, that you may see. As many as I love, I rebuke and chasten. Therefore be zealous and repent. Behold, I stand at the door and knock. If anyone hears My voice and opens the door, I will come in to him and dine with him, and he with Me. To him who overcomes I will grant to sit with Me on My throne, as I also overcame and sat down with My Father on His throne. He who has an ear, let him hear what the Spirit says to the churches"'" (Rev. 3:14–22).

It was just like looking over the edge of the world!

We were swimming outdoors in one of a number of huge cisterns into which had once cascaded warm spa water, pushed up to the surface by hot springs. There at Heirapolis, leaning over the edge of the white, calcium-covered cistern, we had a view across the beautifully green, expansive valley that lay far below us and stretched twenty miles down to Colossae. The setting sun was an unbelievable glowing red as it sank behind the jagged mountains and cast a shadow over a small, unnaturally symmetric hill rising out of the plateau below.

THE LAODICEAN SITE

From that vantage point, and in that glorious setting, we were looking at the site of Laodicea, now completely covered with the dust and rubble of time—and, because of its inaccessibility, unlikely to be excavated. We had visited the site earlier in the day and spent an hour tracing all that remains of the city; the stadium of Domitian, now completely overgrown, and the most fascinating remains of a water pumping station, its many pipes encrusted with calcium.

That area is known for its many hot springs, and the Laodiceans had harnessed the supply and fed it through pipes to various parts of the city. From the Laodicean site the view across the valley to the city of Heirapolis is stunning. The calcium, deposited by the spa water as it cascades down the hillside, glistens sparkling white in the sunshine and resembles huge ridges of snow waiting patiently to melt in the sun.

There is no evidence that the spa water was ever channeled across the valley to Laodicea, but there can be no question that in His message to the church there, Jesus drew imagery from that site, which could be seen clearly from the city of Laodicea. No Laodicean Christian could fail to see the implications of the message, and those springs were the trademark and visual aid the Lord used to press home His invitation.

It is not surprising, amid all that beauty, that Jesus introduced Himself as "the Beginning of the creation of God" (Rev. 3:14). He who was in the beginning was speaking to a church surrounded by the majesty of creation. Laodicea was hemmed in by magnificently rugged mountains, a gloriously green valley, and a breathtaking view of the waterfalls at Heirapolis. Surely they were beneficiaries of the handiwork of God!

CLUES FROM HISTORY

How gracious is the Lord God that from the material of everyday life He draws analogies to help us learn and remember! That is why things like bread and wine are the stuff of which sacraments are made. The first and most obvious historical connection is the mention in verse 15 of their works being neither hot nor cold. The nature of the spa water is that it is lukewarm, rather bitter in taste, and, when consumed in any quantity, can produce nausea, as some of us discovered.

Another allusion Jesus made was to the natural calcium, which was chipped from the surface of the rock and ground into a powder for use as an eye salve (see v. 18). Indeed, a quite reputable medical school developed around the waterfalls, using natural salts, the eye ointment, and spa water baths as part of the cures. Not least, the water was good for cleaning the black wool from the long haired sheep specially reared in the valley and for washing cloth strips for sale as white garments—indeed the properties in the spa water of Laodicea made even the whitest garment look whiter! (v. 18).

All that activity, of course, brought added trade to Laodicea, already on the trade route from Antioch to the west. The citizens were proud of their beautifully natural surroundings and the skills with which they had improved their lives. Certainly they had every reason to be proud. A reputable medical school; a major commercial investment in the wool trade (the soft black wool being woven into special lengths and sent down the trade routes for shipment from Ephesus or Smyrna to all parts of the empire); and many possibilities from the harnessed hot water supplies in their own city—all these conspired to expand the greatness of Laodicea.

The major highways of trade converged at Laodicea, making the city a center for finance and commerce beyond its already natural viability. It was a gathering place for the wealthy and influential, who either had homes there or visited "to take the spa waters." There was a theater, a stadium, a fully equipped gymnasium, an underground central hot water system heating most homes and providing pleasant public baths.

The city was so wealthy, in fact, that when Rome wanted to send aid to rebuild the city after an earthquake, the city fathers graciously waived the offer aside, preferring to pay their own bills!

And among those exquisite surroundings God planted a church. It was a church that became so caught up in its surroundings that Jesus accused them, "You say, 'I am rich, have become wealthy, and have need of nothing'" (Rev. 3:17).

This was a listless Christian community. Like its famous spa water, it was neither hot nor cold. If the people had been cold, God could have warmed them to life. If they had been too hot, God could have cooled them down, guided and used them. But they were lukewarm, and God could only spit them out of His mouth. My suspicions are that those believers were unbearable to know. So arrogantly wealthy, they applied their prosperity only to themselves and to their own needs. So pitifully blind to their sickness, they even prided themselves in the belief that their prosperous self-indulgence was a sign of God's special blessing. No wonder they made Him sick!

GROWING INTO RICHNESS

To the destitute but faithful Christians at Smyrna, Jesus had said that their faith and endurance made them rich. To the abundantly rich believers at Laodicea, so dependant on their financial ability to fix things and be in need of nothing, Jesus says they are in fact poor, blind, wretched people (see v. 17).

Catherine de Hueck Doherty has given us a prophetic picture of what happens when a church perceives prosperity as being of first importance in the self-sufficiency stakes. It becomes self-indulgent and loses its vision. She writes,

> This is no time to be worrying about our images. This is no time for religious orders to be building million dollar plants and $75,000 altars. This is the time for becoming a Christian in the fullness of that simple phrase 'followers of Christ.' To each and every one of us, no matter what our state in life, Christ's life stands as our example. All we have to do is to translate it for all to understand. Only love can do this.[1]

Many Christians at Laodicea, blinded by their own prosperity, would not understand this kind of language. Love is self-denying, and it was an absence of that attitude of love that Jesus was calling into question. The arrogant pride in assuming that wealth could solve all of their problems had tended to make them become dependent upon it to "get

---

[1]Catherine de Hueck Doherty, *The Gospel Without Compromise* (London: Collins, 1979) p. 11.

things done." Such prosperity only made God obsolete. And it was this dependence on their ability and prosperity that rendered them "wretched, miserable, poor, blind . . ." (v. 17).

The way we view God affects theology. When a church has the ability and finances to make things happen, it can be imagined that even God can be helped along—He is presented with ministries, buildings, often excessive staff membership, and then invited to bless the plans. You see, when we can afford to "buy ministry," we often try to manipulate God rather than discover His ways. How poor we can become!

Picture a young lad at school, a faithful Christian, eager to witness, disciplined in his devotion to Jesus Christ. He goes off to college where his faith is strengthened as he shares fellowship and ministry with other Christians. He graduates and moves on to a profession and up the promotion ladder. Out comes the attaché case and smart suits; up goes his mortgage and lifestyle; down goes his trust in the Lord as he manages more and more income; and out goes his time with God's people. Now he can help the Lord with his new money and influence. He's too busy to go to church for worship but he encourages his wife and family and pays his dues.

His enthusiasm for Jesus is neither hot nor cold. Now he has a sophisticated set of questions. Now he can afford to manage his life, and God can be freed to spend time with others! He will help see to it that the church will be financially in need of nothing.

I've never known a Christian to make a decision *not* to follow Christ, but have often observed them simply grow lukewarm. It is a pattern as regular as clockwork. Personal prayer begins to disappear, that implicit trust in Jesus becomes a guarded trust backed by "contingency plans," and commitment to God's people wanes.

Something of a similar spiritual decay had been taking place among Christians at Laodicea. Long before Jesus told them they were lukewarm and nauseous, they were a gathered community of the self-sufficient!

DIVINE COUNSEL

Against this backdrop of a church blind to its own needs, Jesus offered special counsel. He presented to them the way back to a healthy spiritual state, again using everyday motifs to press home His invitation: "I counsel you to buy from Me gold refined in the fire, that you may be rich; and white garments, that you may be clothed . . . ; and anoint your eyes with eye salve that you may see" (v. 18). Whereas we might be tempted to lose patience and write off these people, Jesus Christ, because of His great mercy, extended even to them a gracious invitation—He would heal. Jesus' nature is to reach into our situation and provide all that is necessary for healthy spiritual life.

So obvious are the allusions, they hardly need explanation. The Laodiceans were accustomed to dealing in gold, and then as now it was a highly priced commodity. It was a barometer of wealth. There is a gold, says Jesus, that money cannot buy: "Buy from Me gold refined in the fire" (v. 18; see Is. 55:1-4; Matt. 13:44). It has been well said that the entrance fee into the kingdom of God is absolutely free—the annual subscription is everything we possess! Total, unconditional surrender to Jesus Christ, the One who became sin for us that we, who are sinners, might be made sinless, is the way to this salvation.

The white garments we have already heard about in the letter to Sardis are the symbol of purity with which Christ clothes believers and makes it possible for them to stand, without guilt, in the presence of a holy God. This symbolism appears frequently throughout Revelation. In this passage, it draws a comparison between the whitening value of the spa waters and the whiteness of garments washed in the streams of salvation—or, as the Revelation says so often, "in the blood of the Lamb" (Rev. 7:14).

The eye salve picture is, of course, very recognizable. Whereas the Laodicean Christians thought themselves to be in need of nothing, Jesus reminded them that there was a gold money couldn't buy; a white garment, whiter than the spa water can produce; and an eye salve of much greater value than the calcium-based ointment of Heirapolis.

Furthermore, Jesus implied that the Christians at Laodicea, who thought themselves in need of nothing, were more desperately blind to their pitiable condition before God than those who came to their eye hospital for treatment with eye salve. Here was a call to begin putting the house in order. And believers are reminded that Jesus will provide all that is needed to put things right.

THE LOVE OF GOD

We need to make an observation here. It was not commerce, wealth, or even influence, that Jesus was rebuking. It was the way in which those things subverted God as the focus of trust in Laodicea, and the subsequent conditions, that Jesus addressed. His counsel was not intended to put them at ease, however, neither was it an angry display of divine condemnation. It was counsel given as an express demonstration of God's love for His people (see v. 19). Its purpose was to create penitence as a way to fellowship with God.

Jesus reminded His people of the consistency of the Father's dealings with His people in just that way. When Moses was instructing the ancient people of God concerning their future in the Promised Land, he recounted a journey through the desert that had taken a whole generation to complete. He was speaking to a generation that had known nothing other than life in the desert.

It had not been intended that way, however. God's original intention had been for that first generation to go into the Promised Land. Instead, because of the rebellious nature of the first generation, it proved to be a long and remarkable journey of hardship and miracle, of doubt and faith, in which, as Moses said,

> "[God] humbled you, allowed you to hunger, and fed you with manna which you did not know nor did your fathers know, that He might make you know that man shall not live by bread alone. . . . Your garments did not wear out on you, nor did your foot swell these forty years. So you should know in your heart that as a man chastens his son, so the LORD your God chastens you" (Deut. 8:3–5).

Can you hear echoes of Moses' speech as Jesus takes up the same theme for Christians at Laodicea? "As many as I love, I rebuke and chasten" (v. 19). How faithful is the Bible to its own record!

Jesus, who loves His people with an everlasting love, did not withdraw His love from Laodicea. Instead He demonstrated it by rebuking them for a mistaken attitude toward wealth and power. He rebuked a church caught up in the worldliness it sought to challenge. He chastened a church enculturated by the culture it set out to redeem. And no true father who loves his child will stand by and do nothing if the child is headlong on a course of self-destruction. He will, instead, reprove and chasten for this very reason; the father cares! "As many as I love, I rebuke and chasten."

It is because he loves his child that a father chastens the toddler playing too dangerously near the fireplace. It is not anger, but love, that motivates a parent to rebuke wrongdoing as a child grows. One only has to deal with the unhappy, rebellious, rootless adult to see that a mushy lack of discipline in childhood replaced the real and directional love of the parent who knows when and how to rebuke. Loving rebuke need not be overly painful when there is always restoration offered.

Jesus, who loves His people with an everlasting love, did not withdraw this love from Laodicea, but opened the way for restoration. "Be zealous and repent" (v. 19), He said. The invitation to discover restoration was coupled with an invitation to deal with lukewarmness of faith, by "turning around." For disaster would be the end result of their lukewarm Christianity.

GOD'S INITIATIVE

Repentance, however, is only the beginning of restoration: "Behold, I stand at the door and knock. If anyone hears My voice and opens the door, I will come in to him and dine with him, and he with Me" (v. 20).

Can there be any greater picture of God's grace and merciful love than this? To a lukewarm church, which deserves only to be cast out, was issued a tender invitation to receive Christ once again. As the parent holds out arms wide to engulf the child after a chastening for being too near the fire, so the heavenly Father stretches out His arms and invites us to come to Him. The initiative is with God, who says, "I am *already* standing at the door, knocking, waiting with a love that will not force itself upon you, but will wait for you to come."

It was an invitation first to a whole church. You see, the

whole church was self-reliant but spiritually lukewarm. God had spoken. He continued to speak: "If anyone hears My voice and opens the door. . . ." To refuse to hear would be a disastrous route (see v. 17); to turn around and follow Jesus meant restoration. Jesus visited this wayward church, in which lukewarm Christianity was as repulsive as the stench of death, and having taken the initiative, waited for the door to open.

When Jesus is left outside the church it becomes corporately wretched, however prosperous it may appear to be (see v. 17). We have already seen in a previous chapter how it is possible to organize a prosperous church, and lukewarmness is the result. David Watson develops this thought in his book *I Believe in the Church:*

> Knowing that it is always God's church can prove a challenge to us. How far are we really depending on Him, trusting in Him, praying to Him for the life and power that we all need? What place has corporate prayer in our fellowship? To what extent do we give ourselves to earnest believing prayer? Or do we, to be honest, conduct our lives and work as though the situation was largely in our hands?[2]

The arms outstretched, inviting restoration, are firstly toward a whole Christian community.

However, a church is made up of individual people. So this invitation is a call to every member to respond, that the promise of renewal might come to the whole company. The spirit of self-sufficiency in Laodicea had taken on corporate dimensions because each member joined together to create that image. Thus, Jesus also called each individual in the church to repentance, one by one: "If *anyone* hears My voice and opens the door, I will come in *to him* and dine

[2]Watson, *I Believe in the Church,* p. 69.

174

with him, and *he with Me*" (v. 20 italics mine). Notice the personalization of the invitation in that text as it echoes Abraham's plea for Sodom in the Old Testament (see Gen. 18:16–33). Abraham pleaded for God to save the city if there were only ten righteous persons in it. Would He also save Laodicea for a few righteous members? Renewal in a lukewarm church can begin when renewal takes place in one lukewarm Christian heart.

The problem in Laodicea appears to stem from the fact that individual Christians had happily substituted corporate prosperity for personal holiness. Depending on their own power, they thought it possible to buy Christian faith and ministry but discovered to their dismay that it was not for sale! Christianity is both personal and corporate, for only when the Christian spends time with Jesus Christ personally in prayer and study can there be any growth, ministry, and life in the church body. I am not talking about created busyness, but true spirituality.

The invitation is to commune with Jesus. Surely it recalls the many times John dined with the Master, until that last supper at which Jesus promised a never-ending communion—". . . I will not drink of this fruit of the vine from now on until that day when I drink it new with you in My Father's kingdom" (Matt. 26:29). To each member of the church who opens the door of his or her life to Jesus, comes an incomparable promise: "I *will* come in to him and dine with him, and he with Me" (v. 20 italics mine).

Only as the heart of a Christian has been opened to the gracious voice of the Lord does this principle of renewed fellowship and ministry become active, because personal holiness will be the gauge to determine the quality of life together in God's church. Recall that it was Saint John who recorded Jesus' teaching to the disciples and must himself have subsequently preached it in Laodicea (and elsewhere):

"You are already clean because of the word which I have spoken to you. Abide in Me, and I in you. . . . for without Me you can do nothing" (John 15 :3–5).

That's the key! "Without Me you can do nothing!" Not all the prosperity in the world, not all the riches, not self-sufficiency, not expertise, can in the end accomplish anything for God. That way is pitiable, wretched, poor, and blind, for it leads only to lukewarmness, even in churches with great potential. Since we can offer God nothing and do nothing without Him, His call is to abide in His love. Renewal cannot be bought or manufactured. It is experienced in the church as individual believers abide in Jesus; and the rewards are great.

THE GREAT WHITE THRONE

"To him who overcomes I will grant to sit with Me on My throne" (v. 21). Overcomes what? In the context, it would appear to refer to overcoming the battle with lukewarm Christianity, which was the result of selfish sinfulness in seeing no further than their own needs. Renewal can be said to be taking place in a church only when it shares its resources outside of itself. The nature of the kingdom of God is for its members to share in the needs of others (see Matt. 25:31–46). When a church is not doing that, and its membership is not personally involved in mission, then selfish Christianity is present and lukewarm faith will be found.

The Christians at Laodicea had plenty of opportunity to share their blessings even in their own valleys. Smyrna would have been appreciative of any help they could get, and Laodicea would surely have heard of their plight through Christians who traveled the trade routes. But the Laodicean church lived for itself—and the church that lives for itself will die by itself. Says Jesus, "Him who overcomes [sin] I will grant to sit with Me on My throne, as I also overcame [sin]" (v. 21).

There is much mention of the great throne in Revelation. It symbolizes the divine seat of all power and authority. Those who abide in Jesus will share His new life with Him. But it is a totally self-giving life. The place of power cannot be bought or earned, but comes through personal communion with Jesus here on earth. And personal communion itself will lead one to discover God's agenda for mission, which will be a life lived in the service of others in the power and for the glory of Jesus Christ.

The great sadness for us is that the Christian church in many places has still not come a great deal further than Laodicea in its spiritual journey. We still worry ourselves about maintenance, expansion, and investing for tomorrow's church far more than about today's mission.

"Let me in," Jesus pleads to a church that is saying, "I am rich, have become wealthy, and have need of nothing."

It is still true that Jesus can "remove your lampstand from its place" (Rev. 2:5), that is, take away a church's privilege of witnessing for Him (see Rev. 1:20). Let us not be so busy proving God's presence with us by pointing to success or prosperity that we fail to notice that Jesus isn't there anymore!

Chapter 10

FROM SAINT JOHN TO NICEA:
The Promise of the Spirit

And they sang a new song, saying:

"You are worthy to take the scroll,
And to open its seals;
For You were slain,
And have redeemed us to God by Your blood
Out of every tribe and tongue and people and nation,
And have made us kings and priests to our God;
And we shall reign on the earth."

Then I looked, and I heard the voice of many angels around the throne, the living creatures, and the elders; and the number of them was ten thousand times ten thousand, and thousands of thousands, saying with a loud voice:

"Worthy is the Lamb who was slain
To receive power and riches and wisdom,
And strength and honor and glory and blessing!"

And every creature which is in heaven and on the earth and under the earth and such as are in the sea, and all that are in them, I heard saying:

"Blessing and honor and glory and power
Be to Him who sits on the throne,
And to the Lamb, forever and ever!"

178

Then the four living creatures said, "Amen!" And the twenty-four elders fell down and worshiped Him who lives forever and ever (Rev. 5:9–14).

The question drums endlessly in our ears, is it ever possible for *any* church to be on target? It is not enough to disarm opposition to the church's glaring sin by saying, as so often is the case, "There is no such thing as a perfect church, and if you find one leave it, for it will have ceased to be perfect."

Does it not amaze you that by A.D. 95, just thirty years after the death of Peter and Paul, and within three generations of the beginning of Christianity, 80 percent of the churches mentioned in the Lycus and Maena valleys were seriously astray in their faith and purpose?

But wait! This also gives us hope! Rather than being cast off, those churches were recipients of divine visitation. They were tenderly admonished, pointed in the way of repentance, and encouraged to faithfulness.

What one picture emerges clearly as the weakness of the church in the 80 percent admonished places of Christianity? It is, for me, a picture of *contrived religion.*

I mean by that, dishonest faith. It tricks, mesmerizes, and dishonestly ushers in to the kingdom of God—by a method, a set of rituals, or an organization—people who want Christianity at their own price or who see Christianity as a new way of escape. It is deathly faith.

To exist, paganism had to contrive "faith" by creating experiences—good feelings—based on minimal factual truth, indeed, no truth at all! These "good feelings" were transferred into the church, as it were, and offered as better "feelings" than those outside it. Whether it was the good feeling of strength in Ephesus or the "deeper" but immoral excesses in Thyatira; the exhilaration of acceptability in Sar-

179

dis or the arrogant self-sufficiency in Laodicea; the good feeling of tolerance in the syncretism at Pergamos or, even in our own day, settling for a contrived religion that asks nothing more than an experience of "good feelings," it all left the church reeling from every wind of doctrine— punch-drunk with a "feelings" religion.

There is no short cut to Christian holiness, either in the individual or in the church! There are movements in the church in the twentieth century which, like those in the first, offer short courses or quick-sure ways to knowing and following Christ, based largely on experience and contrived religion. Their organizers may sincerely want to further the ministry of the gospel, but that way is always one of defeat, for it keeps people ignorant of the truth and prolongs immaturity of faith. I suspect the churches in Asia Minor were intent on making the gospel palatable or helping people to be excited about their faith, but contrived religion will always be short-lived and in the end will create more confusion than solution.

Saint Paul's own response to Corinth, a church very much in tune with "good feelings" and contrived religion, keeps flashing to my mind:

> Therefore, having this ministry by the mercy of God, we do not lose heart. We have renounced disgraceful, underhanded ways; we refuse to practice cunning or to tamper with God's word, but by the open statement of the truth we would commend ourselves to every man's conscience in the sight of God. And even if our gospel is veiled, it is veiled only to those who are perishing (2 Cor. 4:1–3 RSV).

The only way Paul and his partners in the faith knew to mature Christians in faith and witness was by open statement of the truth and by lives which commended themselves in the sight of God. Only in that light, now as then, can the Christian live with the (often hard) truth that if the gospel is veiled or hidden, it is so only to those who are perishing because of their refusal to see.

Contrived religion only becomes attractive when the church is uncomfortable with its apparent "weakness" in the world. If the way of justifying one's own "weakness" is to then offer "strength" through experiences, or opportunities for good feelings as a sign of faith, the church is at the mercy of all kinds of dangerous personalities and activity. Good feelings and experiences are not the basis of Christian faith and, when activated without a bedrock of biblical truth, they can be disastrous. Such were the churches pastored by Saint John. They had laid aside the truth for their own convenience, and in the name of love offered immaturity in Christ as the alternative.

Picture the scene one Sunday morning in that first century as Christians in the valley begin to slip out of their houses and, almost furtively, gather together in the home designated for that Sunday's meeting. Some are huddled together in places they try to keep secret. In other cities they move quite freely to homes known to the civil authorities.

There is great interest as it is announced that a letter, which has arrived from their exiled bishop, will be presented as the teaching for that day. As the opening words are read, which presently form the first chapter of the Revelation, they firmly nod in agreement. This is surely a word from the Lord! They thrill to phrases like, "To Him who loved us and washed us from our sins in His own blood, and has made us kings and priests to His God and Father, to Him be glory and dominion forever . . ." (Rev. 1:5–6).

They recognize John's self-evident portrait: "I, John, both your brother and companion in tribulation, and in the kingdom and patience of Jesus Christ, was on the island that is

called Patmos for the word of God and for the testimony of
Jesus Christ" (Rev. 1:9). And they settle down to listen.

A CORRECTIVE BLESSING

The faithful listen with readiness. Those who have been
contriving religion and settling for some way to make Christianity palatable are going to be shocked, though they do
not know it yet.

The first thing the letter says is that the purpose of the
prophecy is blessing to those who read it in the church and
to those who will listen (see 1:3). Events must soon take
place about which Jesus wants His servants to be aware.

We may only surmise that those "events" were disorder
in a church attempting to accommodate the gospel to the
hostile culture around them. Greater wars were going to
rock the empire and Christians needed to get their spiritual
house in order, personally, if they were to deal effectively
together with persecution and pain. So Jesus sent this
prophecy through John, meant for their blessing.

Jesus never deals with His followers to harm or torment
them. The truth is, Jesus has a word of encouragement
even in his stern directions because, as humility recognizes, repentance is the way to life and blessing.

The second thing we should notice about the letter is that
Jesus revealed himself to John in phrases pregnant with
meaningful illustration for each place; they acted like famil-
iar calling cards. Compare the references! Stars and can-
dlesticks for the orthodoxy of Ephesus (see 1:13,16; 2:1); for
the suffering and defeated Smyrna, He is the One who was
dead and came to life (see 1:18; 2:8); to the church at Pergamos, surrounded by civil authority, He comes with a two-
edged sword (see 1:16; 2:12); in opposition to the god of
Thyatira, Jesus is described as One with eyes like a flaming

fire and feet of burnished bronze (see 1:14,15; 2:18); for Gnostic Sardis, Jesus has the seven Spirits from God (see 1:16; 3:1); for powerless Philadelphia, He holds the keys (see 1:18; 3:7); and to arrogant Laodicea, Jesus is the First and the Last (1:17; 3:14).

John's vision reveals this magnificent, awesome, terrible person, who describes Himself as the First and the Last, the One who died and is alive forever more, the One who has the keys of death and hell. He recognized Jesus!

John got the picture! I am sure his fellow Christians on the mainland received it too. Jesus was alive. He was moving actively among the churches. But why those seven? Likely because they were John's charge. As overseer he had already recognized some of the problems Jesus isolated. Perhaps the seven were all linked as churches established out of Ephesus, as the apostles and elders moved up and down the trade routes. Jesus spoke to the believers, telling them that He was present, reigning as Lord. His angels were ready to do His bidding.

Our final picture of Jesus in the Bible, then, is not the cross, the empty tomb, or even the Ascension—all glorious truths of the gospel. Our new picture is one as much for the final days of the church as it was for the first days—Jesus is alive and present among His people! He is moving among the churches that bear His name, to bless, encourage, reprove, and guide.

Would the word of Jesus be welcomed by the Christians who gathered to hear John's letter read to them on that Lord's Day? As we return to the scene, there is a great sense of excitement as each place hears its name and recognizes the motif. But now come the messages. Some parts will be recognizable to members in all the churches, some will certainly come as a sobering reproof, some as a great surprise.

Everyone knows about the pain of being a Christian in Pergamos. The compromise controversy at Thyatira has probably raised some eyebrows. Perhaps there is surprise that Jesus is not impressed with the go-ahead church at Sardis, and that He disowns the claim to His blessings at Laodicea. But what about faithful Smyrna, or "weak" Philadelphia—those churches who love God but cannot impress the world? And how do they handle the comments about the Nicolaitans, or the tolerant sophistication of the Balaamite heresy, or the experiential faith of the Jezebel in Thyatira? And how do the Christians at Sardis react to the news that their reputation for being alive was death in Jesus' eyes?

I dare say there was some controversy among the seven sister churches. Those who had tried to be faithful to what they had heard and received concerning Jesus, found words of encouragement and commendation.

Those churches that had created their own theology on the flimsiest of Christian truth, as a way of making the gospel more palatable, were given clear directions about rectifying the situation. And I have no doubt some left the church offended by John's preaching! "He's too narrow, too harsh, and too judgemental," they would cry. Perhaps they also thought him too simplistic.

But the directions are themselves cause for optimism. If churches repent and conquer through Christ they will find acceptance. They will discover new joy and blessing when they recognize that He is among His church to defend and strengthen, He who is "the ruler of the kings of earth" (Rev. 1:5), who "is coming with the clouds, and every eye will see Him, and they also who pierced Him. And all the tribes of the earth will mourn because of Him" (Rev. 1:7).

JESUS IS LORD

There is reason for confidence! As the letter is read and the things that shall be are revealed (see 4:1), there come other reasons for faith and optimism in the church.

One of them is in chapter 5 where the gospel account of the cross is retold, this time from heaven's gallery. We are introduced to a scene where a Lamb, who had marks "as though it had been slain" (5:6), was standing on a throne ready to break the seals on a scroll that would reveal things to come. Those events, though immediately affecting the believers in John's day, have timeless significance. The scene reveals Christ as Victor, and knowing this prepares and encourages Christians to repent and trust Christ, who is Head of the church and reigns victoriously over all things.

Though there are undoubtedly many other reasons for optimism in the church, the one I want to highlight is in chapter 12. There has been a war in heaven, we are told, which one recognizes as having been played out on earth in the real-life drama at Calvary. The story reveals Jesus as the risen King. Whatever the dragon of chapter 12 (the Devil, the empire, the hostile world) may do, it is but a listless swishing of the tail. If you remain faithful, says John, he cannot do you any lasting harm. Kill you, perhaps. But not lasting harm!

THE FINAL WARNING

What did the Christians of Asia Minor do with all this? Their immediate response, of course, is not on record but that strange mixture of manmade theology, directing God's self-revelation to suit human whims and fancies, did not entirely disappear. Neither may it be said that succeeding generations, even to the present day, have taken the messages seriously. Perhaps *that* is why the following warning appears at the close of the book: "For I testify to everyone who hears the words of the prophecy of this book: If anyone adds to these things, God will add to him the plagues that are written in this book; and if anyone takes away from the words of the book of this prophecy, God shall take away his part from the Book of Life . . ." (Rev. 22:18–19).

Was that really just a defensive, hands off, frightener added later, as some suggest, or a warning that even as the prophecy came some would want to tamper with it and change it to suit their own ends? People would certainly read into it their own hidden secrets and eventually create some kind of universal religious mixture of it. Indeed, history would suggest that this is exactly what happened to the syncretistic, private theology permeating the seven churches.

For example, the evil mixture of paganism, and a misunderstanding of Judaism and Christianity, formed Islam and found an easy-mark audience in the pluralism of Asia Minor. The stranglehold of the minaret replaced the cross and its gospel of freedom in Christ. By the twelfth century, Islamic militancy conquered the Middle East in an empire that spread as far as Israel. Indeed it was the strength of Islam in Israel, especially Jerusalem, that gave rise to the Crusades, as did the offense of a Mosque built on the very site of the temple. Only in ancient Smyrna (Izmir) does the Christian church oust the mosque today, and even there it is under pressure. Islam is still on the move, and it benefits from disenchanted seekers after faith who find Christianity a privatized and contrived religion.

WHERE JESUS WAS DECLARED TO BE GOD

From the start the Bible and faithful Christians never doubted the full divinity and humanity of Jesus Christ. The Scriptures assume it. The apostles taught it. The faithful early Christians believed it.

As time went on, however, the enemy created problems, some of which presented themselves in very practical ways in the churches of the Roman provinces. Peter, Paul, and John all dealt with these issues in their epistles. By the time the Revelation was penned, only two churches in the area of Asia Minor received unconditional praise from Christ, and that was for people who did not doubt His divinity. Both churches were under persecution and forged their faith on an altar of fire. The other five suffered from internal decay and did so because they tried to rearrange the impossible story of the God-man by presenting a harmless Christianity that was acceptable to the culture in which they found themselves. How they tried to streamline the gospel into a palatable religion is seen in the reduction of doctrine, and in the substitution of emotion and "good feelings" for Christian experience.

Problems continued to arise in the early centuries of the church, usually around the Person of Jesus Christ. Is He fully God and fully man at once? People were establishing themselves as recipients of special revelation, forcing the church into decisions she did not want to make. Some were simply leading Christians away from the church to follow doubtful people and doctrines and there was much heresy and privatized theology.

All this was reminiscent of those early seeds of error sown in Asia Minor which John found himself addressing in his letter. John did not pick out "wrong things" in the church in order that he could attack them. That is judgementalism. Instead he preached truth about the Christian faith, and that threw into relief error. Preaching truth is the only way to deal with error in the church. By the late second century, error had many grandchildren because, presumably, not many pastors were preaching truth.

In the year A.D. 325 a conference of three hundred eighteen bishops met together and formulated a normative statement of apostolic and biblical belief. The conference was held at a church in Nicea and produced a glorious creed which has been the Magna Charta of the Christian Church ever since. It is called the "Nicene Creed."

It was on a recent tour that we came to Iznik, near Istanbul. It was out of the way for our schedule, but we were told that Iznik was the modern name for Nicea. So we took the detour. We wanted to find the ancient church, though our first inquiries in the town proved disappointing. Then a policeman told us that a museum in the town had been both a church and mosque in its day; perhaps that was the place.

There was no roof on the museum, though the architecture suggested an early basilica. The spire had collapsed and at its base was an enormous stork's nest. Once inside the church, we discovered this was an eighth-century church built on a third-century foundation. And indeed, at one point below ground level, on the original foundation walls was a fresco of *Christos Pantokratōr* ("Christ, Ruler of the Universe") from a much earlier period than the eighth century.

This was the church of Nicea! Now decayed, but built on the foundations and in the style of the church in which the 318 bishops had met and formulated the creed which has forever enshrined the Church's confession that Jesus is God. Being in this place was a precious moment for us. I remember calling some of the group together and under the open skies, God's canopy for this church, reading from Revelation 4:11: "You are worthy O Lord,/To receive glory and honor and power;/For You created all things,/And by Your will they exist and were created."

And we recited the Nicene Creed:

We believe in one God, the Father Almighty, Maker of heaven and earth, of all things visible and invisible; And in one Lord Jesus Christ, the only-begotten Son of God, begotten from the Father before all time, Light of Light, true God of true God, begotten, not created, consubstantial with the Father, through Whom all things came into being, Who for us men and because of our salvation came down from heaven, was made flesh by the Holy Spirit and the Virgin Mary and became man. He was crucified for us under Pontius Pilate, and suffered and was buried, and rose on the third day, according to the Scriptures, and ascended to heaven, and sits on the right hand of our Father, and will come again with glory to judge the living and the dead. His Kingdom shall have no end; And in the Holy Spirit, the Lord and giver of life, Who proceeds from the Father, Who is worshipped and glorified together with the Father and Son, Who spoke through the prophets; And in one, holy, catholic and apostolic Church. We confess one baptism for the remission of sins. We look forward to the resurrection of the dead and the life of the world to come. Amen.

God created all things and He is in full control. Nothing happens without His knowledge. He's never taken by surprise. How different things might have been if all the seven churches in this Roman province had trusted in the truth, and instead of doing God's work in their own way, had allowed Jesus to do it in His. What a different story there might have been to tell of their ministry!

And what will history record any differently concerning

the church at the close of the twentieth century? The war in heaven is over and Jesus is Victor. But the twentieth-century church, like its first century counterpart, remains in real danger of being its own worst enemy. For it, too, creates a manmade theology in which buzz words, contrived religion, and "good feelings" are being offered to ease pain, heighten emotions, and attempt to make the church acceptable in human eyes.

We desperately need to repent, to turn to Christ again in humility and faith, and to rediscover how Jesus deals with unbelief and weak faith. May God give us in our day the grace to see Jesus, instead of human empires, as the beginning and completion of our faith. May He give us grace to see Jesus, crowned with glory and honor, moving among the churches still, ready to bring correction, and the benefits of His eternal glory. The battle is His—we share the victory.

GOD'S DYNAMITE

That's all very well, but *how*? How do we share in that victory? How do we see it happening? Have you ever pondered the outpouring of the Holy Spirit upon the apostles at the day of Pentecost (see Acts 2)? John was there, by the way. Have you ever asked yourself what was different? The power of God had appeared as flames of fire and as a mighty rushing wind before that time. Even the ecstatic experiences were not new.

Then what was new? A group of people who, in their own day and age, were discovering for themselves the power of God's dynamite, His *dunamis*, in the Person of the Holy Spirit. *He* would lead them into all truth. *He* would convict the world of sin, of righteousness and of judgement. *He* would lead them into worship and praise, into ministry and witness. They could relax in Christ; they could come out of hiding; they could put aside effort and much activity defending God; they now knew that God would bring ministry to them and draw across their path those who were being saved.

There was no need for religious trickery, contrived worship, or creating good feelings, because they could preach the open statement of the truth; Jesus is Lord:

"For You were slain,
And have redeemed us to God by Your blood
Out of every tongue and people and nation,
And have made us kings and priests to our God;
And we shall reign on the earth" (Rev. 4:9–10).

When that great preacher, Dr. Martyn Lloyd Jones, left an excellent medical practice in London's Harley Street early in his career to pastor an unknown church in a coal valley in Wales, it was for him the only step he could take because he knew himself to be called to preach the truth. His biographer recalls a newspaper report on his first appearance on the platform of his little church:

If in the future he stood in the pulpit, and there was one in the church to listen to him, he would still go on. He had no use for the type of man who was always trying to produce a revival. . . . No man had ever produced a revival, and he was not foolish enough to think or hope for a moment that anything he said would produce such an effect, but he hoped to live in such a way that if, and when a revival came through the grace of God from heaven, they would be worthy of it. That was the spirit in which he took up the ministry.[1]

[1] I. H. Murray, *The Life of D. M. Martyn Lloyd Jones—The First Forty Years; 1899–1939* (Edinburgh: Banner of Truth, 1983) p. 129.

Dr. Martyn Lloyd Jones went on to have a worldwide ministry, which has been instrumental in more lives than we shall ever know, by carefully and patiently preaching the truth of the Scriptures and letting God do His own work. Wales was kept from communism by his preaching ministry.

How does the Christian relax and let God be God? How do we best fulfill our ministry? How are we best prepared for revival? No better words than Charles Wesley's hymn "Jesus, Lover of My Soul" could sum it up; no better words turn us away from our own efforts and back to the Source of all spiritual might, to a rediscovery of His ministry to the world, and to us.

> Thou, O Christ, art all I want;
> More than all in Thee I find;
> Raise the fallen, cheer the faint,
> Heal the sick, and lead the blind.
> Just and Holy is Thy name;
> I am all unrighteousness.
> False and full of sin I am;
> Thou art full of truth and grace.

God has no grandchildren. He is raising to Himself sons and daughters for glory. Our work is simply to rest in Him and know the power of His grace at work in us to will and to do His good pleasure.

As the Greeks said when they came to Philip, people still say, "We wish to see Jesus" (John 12:21). People *still* want to see Jesus. Can you let Him speak for Himself? Can you dare to trust Him to renew His church?

He who testifies to these things says, "Surely I am coming quickly." Amen. Even so, come, Lord Jesus! (Rev. 22:20).

Appendix A

FROM JESUS
TO JUSTIN MARTYR
A.D. 30 to A.D. 165

Year (A.D.)		Events in Church History
	30	Crucifixion and resurrection of Jesus Christ
ROMAN EMPERORS		
37–41 CALIGULA emperor		
41–54 CLAUDIUS emperor		Jews expelled from Rome
	c51	Paul at Corinth
		FIRST MAJOR PERSECUTIONS BEGIN
54–68 NERO emperor Great fire of Rome Petronius writes	62	Death of James, the Lord's brother
	c66	Deaths of Peter and Paul
	66	Great Jewish Revolt against Rome
FLAVIAN EMPERORS		
69–79 VESPASIAN emperor 70 Destruction of Jerusalem		Persecutions a fixed but unwritten policy

72 Last stand of the
zealot band at
Masada

79–81 TITUS emperor
79 Eruption of
Vesuvius at
Pompeii

81–96 DOMITIAN emperor

SECOND MAJOR
PERSECUTIONS BEGIN
95 John exiled to Patmos
96 First Epistle of Clement

96–98 NERVA emperor
98–117 TRAJAN emperor
Tacitus writes
Juvenal writes

(?) Papias (?) *Didache*
c110 Ignatius goes to Rome
c112 Pliny in Bythinia

THE ANTONINES

THIRD PERSECUTIONS

117–138 HADRIAN emperor
135 Revolt of Bar
Cochba

Barnabas (?) 2, Clement,
Hermas
Justin's dialogue with Trypho

138–161 ANTONIUS PIUS

c140 Marcion at Rome
Aristides Apology
c156 Martyrdom of Polycarp
c160 Beginnings of
Montanism
c165 Death of Justin Martyr

Appendix B—A SURVEY OF THE SEVEN CHURCHES

CHURCH	CITY FEATURES	JESUS DESCRIBED	COMMENDATIONS	CONDEMNATION	REMEDY	PROMISE	ANALYSIS
EPHESUS	Many temples; Diana worship; As-size town; Library of Celcus	Holds seven stars and walks among seven lampstands	Hard work, patience, pure doctrine	Lost their love for Jesus	Repent or lose the lampstand	Tree of Life	Internal decay through wrong priority
SMYRNA	High hill is called "Crown of Pagos"; a Roman garrison; a sophisticated place of government	First and Last who was dead and came to life	Faithful under persecution, slander, and opposition	None	None	Be faithful unto death and receive a crown of life	External persecution
PERGAMOS	Major place for emperor worship; many altars; an ancient healing center	With two-edged sword	A faithful church under pressure in society	Tolerated false teaching in the church, to keep peace	Repent, or Jesus will use the sword	Hidden manna and stone with a name on it	Internal decay due to compromise

CHURCH	CITY FEATURES	JESUS DESCRIBED	COMMENDATIONS	CONDEMNATION	REMEDY	PROMISE	ANALYSIS
THYATIRA	A potters town, a buffer town to Pergamos	Eyes like a flame of fire, feet of brass (as their god Apollos)	Busier than ever with much love, faith, patience, and service	They encouraged a person with immoral life and false teaching	Whole church to repent	Power over the nations and the morning star	Internal decay from spiritual indiscipline
SARDIS	Gymnasium, a school, a good site, synagogue	Seven Spirits and seven stars	Nothing good to say; but some praise for those who had not "soiled their garments"	Reputation for being alive while actually dead	Hold fast to Christ and repent	A white robe and name confessed before Father	Internal decay through trust in reputation
PHILADELPHIA	Geophysical area; much instability	Holy and true, holding the key of David	Faithfulness, with trust in God even when weak	None	None	A pillar in God's temple	External pressure, slander, and powerlessness
LAODICEA	Hot springs, healing clinic; financial center	Amen, Faithful and True Witness	None	To be spit out of God's mouth	Repent, and discover Jesus	Fellowship with God	Internal decay through pride and self-sufficiency

BIBLIOGRAPHY

Allen, R. *Missionary Methods; St. Paul's or Ours*. Grand Rapids: Eerdmans, 1979.

Barclay, W. *Letters to the Seven Churches*. London: SCM, 1958.

———. *Educational Ideals in the Early Church*. Grand Rapids: Baker, 1980.

Barth, K. *Dogmatics in Outline*. New York: Harper and Row (Torch Books), 1959.

Bettenson, H. *Documents of The Christian Church*. London: Oxford University, 1963.

Bonhoeffer, D. *The Cost of Discipleship*. New York: Macmillan, 1963.

Bruce, F. F. *Paul—Apostle of the Heart Set Free*. Grand Rapids: Eerdmans, 1980.

———. *The Apostolic Defense of The Gospel*. London: Inter-Varsity, 1976.

Brueggemann, W. *The Prophetic Imagination*. Philadelphia: Fortress, 1978.

Doherty, C. de H. *The Gospel Without Compromise*. London: Collins, 1979.

Drane, J. *Paul*. Tring, Herts (U.K.): Lion Books, 1976.

Freire, P. *Pedagogy of the Oppressed*. New York: Seabury, 1968.

Green, E. M. B. *Evangelism in the Early Church*. Grand Rapids. Eerdmans, 1980.

Hendrikson, W. *More Than Conquerors*. Grand Rapids: Eerdmans, 1964.

Hughes, P. E. *Theology of the Reformers*. Grand Rapids: Baker, 1980.

Kepler, T. S. *Dreams of the Future*. Guildford, Surrey (U.K.): Lutterworth, 1963.

Kung, H. *The Church*. New York: Doubleday, 1976.

Moltmann, J. *Church in the Power of the Spirit*. New York: Harper & Row, 1977.

Nesbitt, M. *Where No Fear Was*. New York: Seabury, 1979.

Packer, J. I. *Knowing God*. Seven Oaks, Kent (U.K.): Hodder, 1973.

Quoist, M. *Prayers of Life*. Plainfield, N.J.: Logos, 1963.

Ramsay, Sir W. H. *The Church and the Roman Empire*. Grand Rapids: Baker, 1979.

————. *Pauline and Other Studies in the Early Church*. Grand Rapids: Baker, 1979.

Smith, M. A. *From Christ to Constantine*. Downers Grove: Inter-Varsity, 1971.

Stott, J. R. W. *Men Made New*. Grand Rapids: Inter-Varsity, 1966.

Trench, R. C. *Commentary on the Epistles to the Seven Churches*. London: Trubner & Co., 1861.

Wand, J. W. C. *A History of the Early Church*. New York: Methuen, 1961.

Watson, D. C. K. *I Believe in the Church*. Grand Rapids: Eerdmans, 1979.

Wilcox, M. *I Saw Heaven Opened*. London: Inter-Varsity, 1975.